CRESCENT CITY SAINTS

CRESCENT CITY SAINTS

Religious Icons
Of
New Orleans

Kevin J. Bozant

Po-Boy Press – New Orleans

CRESCENT CITY SAINTS
Religious Icons of New Orleans

No portion of this book may be reproduced in any form, analog or digital, without written permission from Po-Boy Press.

Text & Photographs
Copyright © 2014 Kevin J. Bozant

poboypress@yahoo.com
www.amazon.com/author/kevinjbozant

All rights reserved

ISBN-13: 978-1494239695

African American New Orleans:
A Guide to 100 Civil Rights, Culture & Jazz Sites
ISBN-13: 978-1466410589

Quaint Essential New Orleans:
A Crescent City Lexicon
ISBN-13: 978-1469951102

Crescent City Soldiers:
Military Monuments of New Orleans
ISBN-13: 978-1449913915

Music Street New Orleans:
A Guide to 200 Jazz, Rock and Rhythm & Blues Sites
ISBN-13: 978-1484944998

Crescent City Saints:
Religious Icons of New Orleans
ISBN-13: 978-1494239695

Cryptic New Orleans:
Cemetery Secrets and Symbols
ISBN-13: 978-1511490023

Rev. G. J. Wegener:
His Life and Ministry in New Orleans
ISBN-13: 978-1981257140

Walking Through New Orleans:
Adventure Afoot
ISBN-13: 978-1721731749

New Orleans Engraved:
Cemetery Elegies and Epitaphs
ISBN-13: 978-1981257584

St. Paul Lutheran Church of New Orleans:
The First 80 Years 1840-1920
ISBN-13: 978-1729200285

www.amazon.com/author/kevinjbozant

DEDICATION

This book is dedicated to my mother
Helen Keim Bozant
for her devotion to her faith,
and dedication to her family.

She is our
Crescent City Saint.

"The saints have always been the source and origin of renewal in the most difficult moments in the Church's history."
- Pope Saint John Paul II

PRELUDE
"Oh, When The Saints Go Marching In."

You will want to be "in that number" when local author Kevin J. Bozant takes you on a spiritual journey to the glorious houses of worship, historic cemeteries, and sacred national votive shrines located throughout various neighborhoods of New Orleans. With the help of over 225 photographs, you will discover the local saints and symbols which give rise to the city's celebrated street names and sanctuaries. St. Roch, St. Anthony, St. Ann, Hope, Piety, Grand Route St. John, Annunciation, Ursulines, and many others are brought to life in the form of mosaics, paintings, statuary, and stained glass. Explore the intricacies of the city's religious traditions including All Saints' Day, St. Joseph's Altars, *making* the nine churches, the living Stations of the Cross, and Voodoo rituals along Bayou St. John.

On this pilgrimage you will visit the National Shrines of St. Ann, St. Roch, Blessed Francis Xavier Seelos, Our Lady of Prompt Succor, The International Shrine of St. Jude, The Grotto and Shrine of St. Frances Cabrini, and the Henriette Delille Prayer Room. Discover why New Orleans is an international destination for travelers seeking spiritual awakening.

A brief discussion of ecclesiastical heraldry reveals the secrets of the Pope's and Archbishop's personal coats of arms as well as the symbolism associated with the Dominicans, Franciscans, Jesuits, and Redemptorists.

This volume also depicts a series of artworks illustrating the life of Jesus Christ as well as a section exploring various manifestations of Our Holy Mother. Throughout this spiritual pilgrimage, you can meditate on each Station of the Cross with examples from 14 prominent New Orleans houses of worship.

FATHER ATHANASE
The Bienville Monument
Bienville Place - Conti and Decatur Streets - French Quarter
Angela Gregory 1955

Father Athanase, a Franciscan friar, acted as guide and spiritual advisor to Jean-Baptiste Le Moyne, Sieur de Bienville. Bienville is recognized as being the Father of New Orleans.

VIA CRUCIS
STATION I

Jesus is Condemned to Death

IMMACULATE CONCEPTION CHURCH
130 Baronne Street - Central Business District

" ... Jesus, you stand all alone before Pilate."

ALL SAINTS' DAY

ALL SAINTS' DAY MASS
The National Shrine of St. Roch - St. Roch Cemetery #1
St. Roch at N. Derbigny Street - Faubourg St. Roch

Growing up in the Ninth Ward of New Orleans, it was not unusual to be spirited away into the mysterious walled cities of the dead to visit a deceased relative on All Saints' Day. The diminutive villages with towering white tombs and peeling plaster were, *where the dead people lived*. Every alley was decorated with bouquets of Chrysanthemums and other colorful flowers. At St. Vincent de Paul Cemetery, we placed flowers on the ancient tomb of my great-grandfather, Reverend G. J. Wegener. We also went around the corner to *visit* Uncle Carl who drowned in the Audubon Park swimming pool in 1944. I never knew either gentlemen, but they were always an essential part of the extended family. All Saints' Day is a significant event in the spectacle of life and death in New Orleans.

The family visit to the neighborhood cemetery on All Saints' Day is a tradition dating as far back as anyone can remember. All Saints' Day is observed elsewhere, but in New Orleans it is ingrained in our spiritual lives as deeply as any other observance on our religious calendar. Weeks prior to All Saints' Day, families clean and limewash their tombs in preparation. Repairs are made if necessary and many families have a picnic lunch on the steps of the tomb.

ALL SAINTS' DAY - November 1, 2006
St. Louis Cemetery #2 - Tremé

This tradition was an annual event for Antoinette K-Doe. Every year on All Saints' Day, she drove K-Doe's van into St. Louis Cemetery #2 and parked it in the same section with Ernie's tomb. She set up a large tent with tables and brought out the cold drinks and large pots of red beans and rice. Food was always available for everyone *visiting* their loved ones.

"It is better to be the child of God than king of the whole world."
- St. Aloysius Gonzaga

SAINT ALOYSIUS GONZAGA S.J.
Immaculate Conception Church
130 Baronne Street - Central Business District

Saint Aloysius Gonzaga is celebrated for his volunteer work among the plague-stricken citizens of Rome in 1591. Six days before his 23rd birthday, he began to show signs of the disease and died shortly thereafter. He is the patron of AIDS sufferers and their caregivers.

The name St. Aloysius is closely associated with 20th century education in New Orleans. Many successful people such as Tom Benson and Richard Simmons attended St. Aloysius High School at the corner of Esplanade and N. Rampart in Tremé. In 1969, the St. Aloysius Crusaders moved to Gentilly to merge with Cor Jesu, forming Brother Martin High School.

SAINT ALPHONSUS de' LIGUORI C.Ss.R.
St. Alphonsus Catholic Church
2030 Constance Street - Irish Channel

Alphonsus Marie Antony John Cosmos Damien Michael Gaspard de Liguori was born near Naples on September 27, 1696. As a 29-year-old priest, Alphonsus de' Liguori faithfully ministered to the homeless in his community. In 1732, he founded the Congregation of the Most Holy Redeemer, better known as the Redemptorists. He endured many years of illness and religious disenchantment. In 1839, he was canonized by Pope Pius VI. Saint Alphonsus is the patron of theologians, perseverance, and honorable people. He is often depicted bent over as a result of the daily pain he suffered from rheumatism.

"At once they left their nets and followed Him."
- Matthew 4:20

SYMBOLS OF SAINT ANDREW
St. Andrew's Episcopal Church
1031 S. Carrollton Avenue - East Carrollton

Andrew was born near the Sea of Galilee and was the first disciple to be called by Jesus. He and his brother, Simon Peter, were fishermen by trade. They left everything behind to follow Christ to become, *fishers of men.*

After the Ascension, Andrew traveled to Turkey and Greece to preach. It is believed that he was crucified in Greece by being bound to an x-shaped cross or *saltire*. Tradition says that he continued to preach for two days from the cross until he expired. The decussate cross, shown in the center of this photograph, is better known as Saint Andrew's Cross.

The fish is an understandable symbol associated with St. Andrew. It also functions as one of the Christian symbols employed by early believers to identify each other. The anchor of hope is also identified with St. Andrew. It is referred to as the mariner's cross.

St. Andrew is the patron of fishermen, sailors, and spinsters.

An old German tradition suggests that if an unmarried woman asks for St. Andrew's help on the eve of November 30, and sleeps naked that night, she will meet her future husband in her dreams.

MOTHER OF THE VIRGIN

SAINT ANN
Holy Name of Jesus Catholic Church
6367 St. Charles Avenue - Audubon

Saint Ann is the beloved Mother of Our Lady and the Grandmother of Our Lord. She is traditionally depicted with a book or scroll as she teaches Mary the significance of the sacred scriptures and the importance of an education. The scroll contains the Ten Commandments and occasionally displays the prophecy of Isaiah 11:1.

ORIGINAL NATIONAL SHRINE OF ST. ANN
2101 Ursulines Street - Tremé-Lafitte

The Original National Shrine of St. Ann in Tremé was founded by the Archconfraternity of St. Ann. The shrine features elements of the Sanctuary of Our Lady of Lourdes Grotto in France, as well as the Holy Stairs of Rome. It was dedicated on July 26, 1902, the feast of Saint Ann.

"Saint Ann, Saint Ann ... Give me a man."

The Shrine of St. Ann is one of several stops on Good Friday in the New Orleans tradition of *making the nine churches*. For young women hoping for marriage, this shrine is a significant part of the journey ending at The National Shrine of St. Roch.

The domain features several statues including St. Ann, The Immaculate Conception, Agony of Jesus in the Garden of Gethsemane, The Crucifixion, and The Resurrection.

*"Father, if Thou are willing, remove this cup from me.
Yet not my will, but Thine be done.
And there appeared to him
an angel from heaven to strengthen Him."*
- Luke 22: 42-43

**AGONY OF JESUS IN THE GARDEN OF GETHSEMANE
Original National Shrine of St. Ann
2101 Ursulines Street - Tremé-Lafitte**

"He has risen - He is not here." - **Matthew 16:6**

THE RESURRECTION OF JESUS FROM THE DEAD
Original National Shrine Of St. Ann
Members of the Archconfraternity of St. Ann
2101 Ursulines Street - Tremé-Lafitte

Group representing the Resurrection of Jesus from the dead: The Risen Savior. Angel with stone rolled away. Roman soldier on guard.
- Monument Inscription

This impressive outdoor sculpture depicts the Risen Savior holding the Christian banner. The banner, which is usually white with a red cross, hangs from a simple, long shaft and crossbar similar to the Roman vexillum. It is Christ's standard and banner representing His victory over death.

The Holy Stairs to the right of the grotto are to be ascended on one's knees with devotion and prayer at each Station of the Cross along the way. The top of the grotto reveals a life-sized depiction of the Crucifixion. Affixed above the head of Jesus is the traditional scroll with the inscription, INRI. The usual figures associated with the Crucifixion group stand at the base of the cross. Mary Magdelen is kneeling at the center. A pitcher of water sits in front of her. Mary, the mother of Jesus, stands to the right of Jesus wearing a robe. John stands to the left of Jesus. All of the figures are painted in bright colors. A plaque reads: *"Woman, behold thy son. Son, behold thy mother."*

Another domain feature is the Cave of Many Shrines where you can pray to the Sacred Heart, Mother of Perpetual Help, Saint Joseph, and Saint Jude. The prie-dieux in the front of the grotto serve as an invitation to kneel and pray with St. Ann and her daughter.

VIA CRUCIS
STATION II

Jesus Carries His Cross

OUR LADY STAR OF THE SEA CATHOLIC CHURCH
1835 St. Roch Avenue - Faubourg St. Roch

" ... the most heavy cross I made for Thee ... "

DOCTOR OF THE CHURCH

SAINT ANTHONY OF PADUA
St. Mary's Italian Church
1116 Chartres Street - French Quarter

Fernando Martins de Bulhões was a Franciscan priest and devoted follower of St. Francis of Assisi. He was declared Doctor of the Church for his oratory as well as his extensive knowledge of the Holy Scriptures.

SAINT ANTHONY OF PADUA

Most images of Saint Anthony feature him wearing his Franciscan habit and cincture while holding a Bible. The Christ Child stands on the open book as though rising from the words on the pages. Other images include St. Anthony holding Jesus while feeding the poor.

An interesting legend surrounds the death of St. Anthony. While his body turned to dust, his tongue remained glistened with a lively red color as if alive and still able to preach. It is still displayed as a relic to this day in Padua.

ST. ANTHONY POOR BOX
St. Anthony Of Padua Church
4640 Canal Street - Mid-City

St. Anthony was canonized on May 30, 1232, and is the patron of Native Americans, animals, fishermen, the poor, and travelers. He is especially called upon when seeking lost articles or people. Saint Anthony is beloved throughout New Orleans and is celebrated by way of St. Anthony of Padua Parish on Canal Street as well as a neighborhood, a school, and a street named after him. Most churches in the city have a statue of St. Anthony which acts as a lost and found department for items left in the pews during worship.

St. Anthony is regarded as a miracle worker or, thaumaturgist. This explains why he is petitioned by New Orleans practitioners of Voodoo in the search for missing people or reconciliation with lost lovers. One calls out the name of St. Anthony, visualizes the lost item, and explains the importance of regaining it. The following prayer is then recited:

"Saint Anthony, Saint Anthony, please come down,
My ____ is lost, and must be found."

In New Orleans, the story is told that Marie Laveau always kept a statue of St. Anthony in her front yard. If the statue was upside down, it was a sign that Laveau was busy at her work and was not to be disturbed.

SAINT ANTHONY OF PADUA
Holy Name of Jesus Catholic Church
6367 St. Charles Avenue - Audubon

Franciscans wear a white cincture around the waist called a *cintura blanca* which means white rope. The knots represent poverty, chastity, and obedience. These are the three cornerstones of the Franciscan Order. The cincture in general is a sign of chastity. St. Dominic also wore the cincture in honor of St. Francis of Assisi. Many confraternities, as well as other groups of those who are faithful to a particular religious cause, wear cinctures as symbols of their affiliation and chastity.

*"... the ever Virgin Mary, having completed
the course of her earthly life,
was assumed body and soul into heavenly glory."*
- ***Munificentissimus Deus***, Pope Pius XII

THE ASSUMPTION OF THE VIRGIN MARY
St. Mary's Italian Church
1116 Chartres Street - French Quarter
Franco Alessandrini - 2002

This magnificent painting of *The Assumption of the Virgin Mary*, by Franco Alessandrini, can be found above the main altar of St. Mary's Italian Church. The Assumption occurred at the end of Mary's earthly life when her body was elevated into heaven. The Virgin Mary's heavenly birthday is observed on August 15, when all believers celebrate that they will also be received into paradise.

SAINT AUGUSTINE OF HIPPO
St. Augustine Catholic Church
Gov. Nicholls and Henriette Delille Streets - Faubourg Tremé

Saint Augustine was willing to view life from many different perspectives resulting in a distinctive approach to theology and philosophy. He was an influential leader in the history of education. Augustine was canonized by popular acclaim and eventually recognized by Pope Boniface VIII as a Doctor of the Church in 1298. He is the patron of brewers and printers. Saint Augustine Church in Tremé and St. Augustine High School in the Seventh Ward are both historic New Orleans institutions named in his honor.

APOSTLE AND MARTYR

SAINT BARTHOLOMEW
Congregazione E. Fratellanza Italiana Di San Bartolomeo AP
Metairie Cemetery - Section 86 - Lakewood
Dedicated March 23, 1884

Bartholomew was one of the Twelve Apostles of Jesus Christ. He was also referred to as *Nathanael of Cana* and apparently martyred in the city of Albanopolis in Armenia. Some accounts suggest that Bartholomew was beheaded, but he is most often represented in religious art as having been skinned alive. In this dramatic stone portrayal, St. Bartholomew is depicted carrying his flayed skin over his right shoulder. His left hand holds a knife, the instrument of his martyrdom. The book represents the Gospel which he introduced to India. He is the patron of tanners and bookbinders. The tomb inscription AP following his name stands for *Apostolo* or Apostle.

BAPTISM

THE CHAPEL OF ST. MICHAEL THE ARCHANGEL
St. Roch Cemetery #2 - Campo Santo
St. Roch at N. Derbigny Street - Faubourg St. Roch

THE SHELL - SYMBOL OF BAPTISM
St. Patrick Cemetery #1 - Mid-City

PATRONESS OF IMMIGRANTS

SAINT FRANCES XAVIER "MOTHER" CABRINI M.S.C.
Harrison Avenue at Canal Boulevard - Lakeview
The Order of the Alhambra - August 25, 1949

This sculpture is a tribute to Saint Frances Xavier "Mother" Cabrini, founding member of the Missionary Sisters of the Sacred Heart. Cabrini arrived in New Orleans in 1892, during a huge influx of immigrants in search of a better life. Their deplorable living conditions worsened during the yellow fever epidemics of 1897 and 1905. Cabrini established two orphanages on Esplanade Avenue. The statue shows Mother Cabrini in full habit with her signature bow tie. Her right hand touches her heart. Her left hand is extended outward slightly, at her side, with palm open and facing outward. The sculpture was a gift to the city of New Orleans from the Order of Alhambra, a fraternal order of Catholic men. The City had to defend its decision to place the religious statue on public land following a lawsuit. An inscription added in 1952 reads: *"Accepted By The City Of New Orleans In Grateful Appreciation Of The Outstanding Civic Work Of Mother Frances Xavier Cabrini."*

This photo was taken a few months after the flooding from Hurricane Katrina. The water line is still visible at her ankles. A nearly identical statue is located on the Cabrini High School campus at 3400 Esplanade Avenue near City Park.

SAINT FRANCES CABRINI GROTTO AND SHRINE
Cabrini High School Campus
3400 Esplanade Avenue - Faubourg St. John

Cabrini's bedroom and the Sacred Heart Chapel are still located on the grounds of Cabrini High School. Born in the Austrian Empire, she was naturalized in 1909, and became the first citizen of the United States to become a saint.

ST. FRANCES XAVIER "MOTHER" CABRINI

URSULINE CONVENT GARDEN
Chartres at Ursulines Street - French Quarter
Franco Alessandrini - White Carrara Marble - 1999

CABRINI HIGH SCHOOL AND ST. AUGUSTINE CHURCH

VIA CRUCIS
STATION III

Jesus Falls the First Time

THE NATIONAL SHRINE OF ST. ROCH
St. Roch Cemetery #1 - Faubourg St. Roch

" ... the heavy burden of my sins is on Thee ... "

VIRGIN AND MARTYR

SAINT CECILIA
Blessed Francis Xavier Seelos Parish Catholic Church
3053 Dauphine Street - Bywater
Original Location: St. Cecilia Catholic Church - Bywater

SAINT CECILIA
Our Lady Star of the Sea Catholic Church
1835 St. Roch Avenue - Faubourg St. Roch

Saint Cecilia promised her virginity to God. When forced to marry, she heard heavenly music inside her heart and was intent on keeping her vows. St. Cecilia is usually depicted playing one of several musical instruments including the harpsichord, flute, organ, harp, or violin. She is the patroness of musicians, church music, and poets. St. Cecilia Catholic Church still stands at North Rampart and France Streets in Bywater. The parish was closed in 2000.

"... And now abideth faith, hope, charity, these three; but the greatest of these is charity." **- 1 Corinthians 13:13**

THE VIRTUE OF CHARITY
**The Cathedral-Basilica of St. Louis King of France
Jackson Square - French Quarter**

Of the Seven Virtues, three are considered to be theological. They are the familiar, Faith, Hope, and Charity. They are traditionally displayed in a grouping of all three. In this setting, they appear high above the main altar of the Cathedral-Basilica of St. Louis. The Virtue of Charity is usually depicted nurturing two children or holding a cornucopia.

SAINT CLARE OF ASSISI
St. Clare's Monastery - 720 Henry Clay Avenue - Audubon

This statue of Chiara Offreduccio rests in a niche on an exterior wall of St. Clare's Monastery. She is wearing a Minorite habit and holding the monstrance displaying the Eucharistic host. This illustrates the time when she warded away the Saracens in the army of the Emperor Frederick II from attacking the Order of San Damiano and saving her sisters from harm. St. Clare was an ardent follower of St. Francis and became the foundress of the order of nuns known as *Poor Clares*. New Orleans was the first permanent home for the order in the United States. They renounce all earthly possessions relying only on God for their livelihood. St. Clare is the patroness of good weather, embroiderers, and television.

"Ego Vos Semper Custodiam" - I will always protect you

Crescent City Saints: Religious Icons of New Orleans

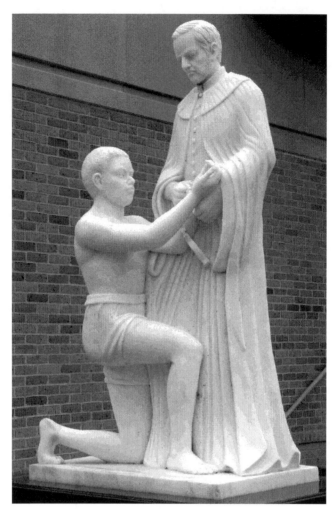

SAINT PETER CLAVER S.J.
St. Peter Claver Catholic Church and School
1923 St. Philip Street - Tremé-Lafitte
Marcus Brown - 2011

Pedro Claver y Corberó was a Spanish, Jesuit priest. He ministered aboard slave ships providing food and healthcare. Pedro Claver personally baptized an estimated 300,000 slaves during his lifetime. Unlike many Jesuits at the time, Claver always treated slaves as fellow Christians. In this moving portrait by Marcus Brown, Claver is removing the shackles from the wrists of a young man. Saint Peter Claver is the patron of slaves, race relations, and African American ministries. The Knights of Peter Claver, the largest African American fraternal organization in the United States, is headquartered here in New Orleans.

PRIEST AND CONFESSOR

SAINT PETER CLAVER S.J.
Blessed Francis Xavier Seelos Parish Catholic Church
3053 Dauphine Street - Bywater

CORONATION OF MARY, QUEEN OF HEAVEN
Court of Our Lady - Queen of Angels Mausoleum
St. Roch Cemetery - Campo Santo
St. Roch at N. Derbigny Street - Faubourg St. Roch
Mosaic Detail - 1964

Purer than Angels, Higher than Archangels, Superior to Principalities, Stronger than the Powers, More excellent than the Virtues, Predominant over the Dominations, More admirable than the Thrones, More beautiful than the Cherubim, More august than the Seraphim.
- **Mausoleum Inscription**

THE VENERABLE HENRIETTE DELILLE

Henriette Delille was born a free woman of color in New Orleans in 1812, and became an prominent social worker and educator. She founded the Sisters of the Holy Family, an African American religious order. Together, with fellow St. Augustine Church member Juliette Gaudin, they cared for the sick, provided shelter for orphans, and gave religious instruction to everyone, both slave and free. The Order of The Sisters of the Holy Family is currently located at 6901 Chef Menteur Highway in the Plum Orchard neighborhood of New Orleans.

PLACE DE HENRIETTE DELILLE
Royal Street at Orleans - French Quarter

In 2010, the Catholic Church declared Delille, *Venerable,* which is two steps away from sainthood. When canonized, she will be the first native-born African American declared a saint by the Catholic Church. She is buried in St. Louis Cemetery #2. In 2011, St. Claude Street in Tremé was renamed in her honor.

HENRIETTE DELILLE PRAYER ROOM
**The Cathedral-Basilica of St. Louis King of France
Jackson Square - French Quarter**

In what was originally the cathedral baptistery, Henriette stood as a godmother to children and adults, slave and free alike. After the baptismal font was relocated to the front of the cathedral, Monsignor Crosby Kern, Rector and devoted member of the Friends of Henriette Delille, secured permission to establish this room as a memorial and prayer room. It was dedicated June 8, 2008.

"I want to live and die for God." - **Henriette Delille**

THE "VENERABLE" HENRIETTE DELILLE
Peter Claver Catholic Church and School
1923 St. Philip Street - Tremé-Lafitte
Marcus Brown - 2011

"Take good care of the service of the poor."
- St. Louise de Marillac

SAINT LOUISE DE MARILLAC D.C.
Blessed Francis Xavier Seelos Parish Catholic Church
3053 Dauphine Street - Bywater

Louise de Marillac was co-founder of the Daughters of Charity with St. Vincent de Paul. Vincent de Paul's guidance strengthened her commitment to caring for the poor, elderly, orphans, soldiers, and those in need of healthcare. She is the patron of social workers, children, the elderly, and widows.

VIA CRUCIS
STATION IV

Jesus Meets His Mother

ST. DOMINIC CATHOLIC CHURCH
775 Harrison Avenue - Lakeview

" ... but it helps to see that she is on your side ... "

PATRON OF THE ARCHDIOCESE OF NEW ORLEANS

SAINT VINCENT DE PAUL C.M.
Catholic Cultural Heritage Center - Ursuline Convent
Chartres and Ursulines Streets - French Quarter

"Evangelizare Pauperibus Misit Me"
He sent Me to Preach the Gospel to the Poor
- Motto of the Vincentians

SAINT VINCENT DE PAUL C.M.
Blessed Francis Xavier Seelos Catholic Parish
Formerly: St. Vincent de Paul Catholic Church
3053 Dauphine Street - Bywater

Saint Vincent de Paul was known as the *Great Apostle of Charity*. He was the founder of the Vincentians, or the Congregation of the Missions. He also co-founded the Daughters of Charity which raised money for victims of war and various missionary projects. De Paul was canonized in 1737, and is the patron of charities, spiritual help, and horses. Blessed Francis Xavier Seelos Catholic Parish in Bywater was formerly called St. Vincent de Paul Catholic Church and there is also a St. Vincent de Paul Cemetery in the Upper Ninth Ward.

THE DOMINICANS

"Laudare, Benedicere, Praedicare" - **To Praise, To Bless, To Preach**

St. Dominic's mother had a prenatal dream that her child was a black and white dog carrying a torch in its mouth which, *"seemed to set the world on fire for Christ."* Black and white are the colors of the order symbolizing truth over heresy. Since dogs are seen as faithful creatures, a pun evolved concerning the term *Dominican*. *Domini* is Latin for Lord and *canis* refers to a dog thus: *Hounds of the Lord*. Dominic of Guzmán established The Order of Preachers. They are also called Blackfriars due to the black cloaks they wear over their white tunics. This architectural detail indicates the principles of the order. The patriarchal cross is surrounded by the crown of glory and eternal blessedness. The shield on the left represents *Veritas* - the truth. The hand forms the sign of the cross and the gesture of the blessing. The right shield reveals the truth and the star or *corona of light* which was emblazoned on Dominic's forehead. The sword represents justice and the torch is a symbol of truth.

ST. ANTHONY OF PADUA CHURCH
Façade Details - 4640 Canal Street - Mid-City

SAINT DOMINIC OF GUZMÁN
St. Dominic Church - 775 Harrison Avenue - Lakeview
Angelo Zarlenga - 1961

Angelo Zarlenga's sculpture depicts a full-length figure of St. Dominic of Guzmán with a star over his head which his godmother saw on his forehead during baptism. The eight points represent the Beatitudes. The Rosary, a gift from Mary, is visible on his left side. He also holds a book in his left hand with his right hand raised over his head. The base features a dog with a torch in its mouth and the Dominican Cross. St. Dominic is the patron of astronomers. This statue was commissioned by Father McMullen.

SAINT KATHARINE DREXEL CHAPEL
Xavier University Campus - Gert Town

As a result of a generous inheritance from her father, Katharine Drexel founded and staffed several educational institutions for Native Americans and African Americans throughout the country. Due to a lack of Catholic education available for African Americans in the South, she came to New Orleans and founded the St. Peter Claver Catholic School in 1921. She and The Sisters of the Blessed Sacrament are credited with having founded Xavier University in the Gert Town neighborhood. Xavier enjoys the distinction of being the only Black and Catholic college in the United States. Drexel is also believed to be the only saint to have founded a university. Many of the Sisters are still active at Xavier, providing staffing and financial assistance. For six decades, Mother Katharine spent nearly $20 million to build churches and schools.

Katharine Drexel was canonized by Pope John Paul II on October 1, 2000. She is one of just a handful of American saints and is the patron of philanthropists and racial justice. A piece of cloth from her habit is kept in the altar of the new St. Katharine Drexel Chapel on the Xavier campus. Xavier University Preparatory School on Magazine Street was recently renamed Katharine Drexel Preparatory School.

This comforting depiction of St. Katharine Drexel, by Marcus Brown, can be found in the courtyard of St. Peter Claver Catholic Church and School in the Tremé-Lafitte neighborhood of New Orleans. She holds an infant in her arm and gently pats the back of a young boy. Drexel, who lived from 1858-1955, dedicated her life to the needs of African and Native Americans. There are several other statues featuring Mother Katharine in New Orleans including one in the Ursuline Convent Garden in the French Quarter. It was sculpted in white Carrara marble by Franco Alessandrini.

"It is for each of us to learn the path by which He requires us to follow Him, and to follow Him in that path." **- St. Katharine Drexel**

SAINT KATHARINE DREXEL S.B.S.
St. Peter Claver Catholic Church and School
1923 St. Philip Street - Tremé-Lafitte
Marcus Brown, Sculptor

ECCLESIASTICAL COATS OF ARMS

"Animam pro ovibus ponere"
To Give One's Life for the Sheep

ARCHBISHOP JOSEPH RUMMEL COAT OF ARMS
Chapel Of The North American Martyrs
Jesuit High School - Pediment Relief Detail
S. Solomon and Palmyra Streets - Mid-City

This beautiful architectural detail depicts Archbishop Joseph Rummel's personal coat of arms. He passed away in New Orleans on November 9, 1964, at the age of 88. Rummel's leadership ended racial segregation in the churches and schools of the Archdiocese. He had a profound impact on education in New Orleans.

There are a number of interesting details associated with ecclesiastical heraldry. There are common elements relating to the title of archbishop, combined with personal symbols including his motto. The shield is the centerpiece of armorial bearings and is surrounded by a variety of external ornaments. Common elements begin at the top with the ecclesiastical hat or pilgrim's galero. The hat varies in color. Green is worn by the archbishop. The galero is laced with a number of knotted cords or tassels. The archbishop has ten.

Above the shield is the processional cross. For an archbishop, the patriarchal cross is employed with its two traverses. The bishop's cross carries one traverse. To the left is the ceremonial headwear or mitre. To the right is a crozier, the pastoral staff. The marshalling of the shield elements does not follow the usual heraldic arrangement in quarters. They are distributed by impalement, or side by side. The seal of the local archdiocese is found on the left, or dexter. The personal symbols chosen by the archbishop are found on the right side of the shield and reflect his particular interests and beliefs. His personal motto is inscribed on the lower banner.

"Deus Providebit" - God Will Provide

ARCHBISHOP JOHN W. SHAW COAT OF ARMS
Notre Dame Seminary Entrance
2901 S. Carrollton Avenue - Marlyville-Fontainebleau

POPE BENEDICT XV COAT OF ARMS
St. Francis of Assisi Catholic Church
631 State Street - West Riverside

It is an 800-year-old tradition for a pope to have his own personal coat of arms. The papal mitre holds three gold crowns representing the three powers of the pontiff including, sacred orders, jurisdiction, and magisterium. Behind the mitre are the traditional crossed keys, one gold and one silver, in the form of St. Andrew's Cross. They are St. Peter's Keys to the Kingdom of Heaven and are symbols of temporal and spiritual power. In the case of Benedict XV, the central escutcheon contains the della Chiesa family arms featuring the imperial eagle and a church.

POPE PIUS XII COAT OF ARMS
Chapel Of The North American Martyrs - Jesuit High School
S. Solomon and Palmyra Streets - Mid-City

Crescent City Saints: Religious Icons of New Orleans

VIA CRUCIS
STATION V

Simon of Cyrene Helps Jesus to Carry His Cross

ST. JOHN THE BAPTIST CATHOLIC CHURCH
1139 Oretha Castle Haley Boulevard - Central City

" ... Blest too shall I be if I aid Thee to bear the cross ... "

THE EUCHARIST

THE CHAPEL OF ST. MICHAEL THE ARCHANGEL
St. Roch Cemetery #2 - Faubourg St. Roch

ST. STEPHEN CATHOLIC CHURCH
1025 Napoleon Avenue - Touro

"The Most Holy Body And Blood Of Christ"

CORPUS CHRISTI
Corpus Christi Roman Catholic Church
2022 St. Bernard Avenue - Seventh Ward
Architectural Detail of Solar Monstrance

The annual Feast of Corpus Christi celebrates the acceptance of the Real Presence of Jesus Christ in the elements of the Eucharist. The mass is often followed by a procession with the traditional solar monstrance, the vessel which contains the host.

CHRIST DISTRIBUTING THE HOLY EUCHARIST
Holy Trinity Greek Orthodox Cathedral
1200 Robert E. Lee Boulevard - Lakeview
Laurence Manos, Iconographer - 1987

SAINT EXPEDITE
Our Lady of Guadalupe (Old Mortuary Chapel)
411 N. Rampart Street - Tremé

SAINT EXPEDITE

"Expedite now what I ask of you.
Expedite now what I want of you, this very second.
Don't waste another day. Grant me what I ask for."

Expeditus was believed to be a Roman centurion who chose to become a Christian and was beheaded during the Diocletian Persecution. Not much is known about Expeditus by the Catholic Church, thus he is not taken as seriously as other saints despite a very devoted following in New Orleans. The widely accepted story associated with Saint Expedite relates to his decision to become a Christian. Satan appeared to Expeditus in the form of a crow insisting that he defer his conversion until tomorrow. Not one to put things off, he stomped on the bird and declared, *"I will be a Christian today!"*

Saint Expedite holds a cross that declares, *hodie*, which is Latin for today. He is generally depicted crushing a crow underfoot with the Latin reference, *cras*, for tomorrow.

America was first exposed to Saint Expedite by way of New Orleans, accompanied by a long-standing legend. When the Old Mortuary Chapel received a shipment of saint statues, one of the crates was unidentified. Only the word *expédit* was visible and the shipping instructions were interpreted as the name of the saint. This story is a bit exaggerated, to say the least, but the anecdote seems to be a favorite among local tour guides.

Saint Expedite remains a very popular saint in New Orleans and is also associated with followers of Voodoo. Practitioners of Voodoo often invoke his intercessions at church or from home on Wednesdays, which is Saint Expedite's Day. It is proper to display a picture of Saint Expedite and light a red seven-day glass candle. Use a green candle if asking for money. The candle is allowed to burn until it goes out and then the glass is filled with water. A bouquet of red flowers is placed in the glass.

In return for his help, you must offer Saint Expedite a slice of Sara Lee pound cake. Any brand of pound cake will suffice, but in New Orleans, Sara Lee appears to get the most expeditious results. Without this essential offering, his favor can disappear just as quickly as it was granted. Saint Expedite's feast day is April 19. He is the patron saint of emergencies and prompt solutions.

"I come to you in need,
Do this for me, Saint Expedite.
And when it is accomplished,
I will as rapidly reply for my part
With an offering to you.
Be quick, Saint Expedite!"
- Prayer to St. Expedite

Crescent City Saints: Religious Icons of New Orleans

"... giving all diligence, add to your faith virtue; and to virtue knowledge ... " - **2 Peter 1:5**

THE VIRTUE OF FAITH
New Orleans Italian Mutual Benevolent Society Tomb
St. Louis Cemetery #1 - Tremé

THE VIRTUE OF FAITH

THE CATHEDRAL-BASILICA OF ST. LOUIS KING OF FRANCE
Jackson Square - French Quarter

ST. PATRICK CEMETERY #2 - MID-CITY

"Oh Holy Saint Florian, spare my house, kindle others."
- The Florian Principle

SAINT FLORIAN
Our Lady of Guadalupe (Old Mortuary Chapel)
411 N. Rampart Street - Tremé

Our Lady of Guadalupe Church is the official church of the New Orleans Police and Fire Departments. Florian von Lorch is depicted as a Roman soldier pouring water over a burning building. Saint Florian is petitioned to protect against fire, floods, and drowning. The official seal of the New Orleans Fire Department is shaped like the Florian Cross.

Crescent City Saints: Religious Icons of New Orleans

VIA CRUCIS
STATION VI

Veronica Wipes the Face of Jesus

ST. AUGUSTINE CATHOLIC CHURCH
1210 Governor Nicholls Street - Tremé

" ... Who didst deign to print Thy sacred face upon the cloth ... "

FRANCISCANS

"Deus Meus Et Omnia" - My God and My All

THE FRANCISCAN ESCUTCHEON
St. Clare's Monastery
720 Henry Clay Avenue - Audubon

Saint Francis of Assisi founded the Order of Friars Minor, also known as the Franciscans. While praying at the church of San Damiano, he heard Christ say to him, *"Francis, repair My Church."* Eventually, Francis realized Christ meant the Universal Church. He instructed his followers to take up the cross daily and renounce all material possessions. He lived for the poor, in fact, as one with them. He became a mentor to Clare of Assisi as she joined Francis in a life of poverty, penance, and seclusion. During his final years he had a vision while praying and received the stigmata, the wounds of Christ. He is the patron of merchants and ecologists.

The Franciscan escutcheon includes two arms crossing each other. The hands display the wounds of the crucifixion. The foreground arm is that of the crucified Jesus Christ. The robed arm is that of St. Francis of Assisi who received the stigmata late in life. This is the traditional symbol of the Franciscans combined here with the Sacred Heart of Jesus, and imagery associated with St. Francis of Assisi's, *Canticle of Brother Sun*.

"Under the Invocation of St. Francis of Assisi"

SAINT FRANCIS OF ASSISI O.F.M.
St. Francis of Assisi Catholic Church
631 State Street - West Riverside
Entrance Tympanum Mosaic Detail

THE ANGEL OF REVELATION

SAINT GABRIEL THE ARCHANGEL
Chapel of St. Michael the Archangel – St. Roch Cemetery #2
St. Roch at N. Derbigny Street - Faubourg St. Roch

The Archangel Gabriel appears in the Bible several times. In Luke 1:13, he appears to Zacharias foretelling the birth of John the Baptist. In Luke 1:31, he appears to Mary prophesying the birth of Jesus - the Annunciation. In Daniel 8:16, he explains Daniel's visions.

SAINT GABRIEL THE ARCHANGEL
Metairie Cemetery - Section 88 - Lakewood
Louis Prima Family Tomb
Alexei Kazantsey - Sculptor

Gabriel is the patron of broadcasters, messengers, and postal workers. He is generally portrayed blowing the sacred horn to wake the dead at the Last Judgment. In this sculpture, Gabriel is depicted blowing a modern Bb trumpet in homage to Louis Prima.

ALMIGHTY GOD

"...and Moses hid his face; for he was afraid to look upon God."
- Exodus 3:6

ST. RITA OF CASCIA CATHOLIC CHURCH
2729 Lowerline Street - Marlyville-Fontainebleau

It is written that no human can behold the face of God and survive. Most sculptors and painters use artistic metaphors for His depiction. A right hand descending from the sky, forming the sign of the blessing, is symbolic of God's intervention in human affairs. He is also frequently depicted as the All-Seeing Eye or the Eye of Providence. The surrounding rays of glory symbolize the Caretaker of humanity watching over His creation.

BASTION FAMILY TOMB DETAIL
Metairie Cemetery - Lakewood

ST. STEPHEN CATHOLIC CHURCH
1025 Napoleon Avenue - Touro

Many *"literal"* portraits of God can be found in New Orleans churches. He is usually included in the depictions of the Baptism of Jesus, the Transfiguration, and the Coronation of Mary.

ST. MARY'S ASSUMPTION CHURCH
919 Josephine Street - Lower Garden District

GOOD FRIDAY

THE STATIONS OF THE CROSS
The National Shrine of St. Roch - St. Roch Cemetery #1
St. Roch at N. Derbigny Street - Faubourg St. Roch

On Good Friday, March 21, 1788, the Great New Orleans Fire broke out less than a block from Jackson Square. Because it was Good Friday, tradition has it that the priests would not allow the church bells to be rung. Most of the buildings in the French Quarter were destroyed, including the church.

Good Friday in New Orleans is steeped in traditions which include *making the nine churches*. The journey was traditionally taken on foot to nine churches in the neighborhood. Meditations on one or two Stations of the Cross are observed at each location. It is often referred to as the Novena of the Nine Churches recalling the trek Jesus Christ took to His crucifixion. It is a way to share the suffering of Jesus by imitating His walk to Calvary.

The term, novena, is derived from the Latin word, *novem*, meaning nine. It is a devotional period consisting of nine days of successive praying. This probably accounts for the number of nine churches. It might also reflect the nine days the apostles spent in Jerusalem awaiting the coming of the Holy Spirit.

There is another long-standing Good Friday tradition in New Orleans. Young women searching for a husband also visit nine churches, say a prayer, and leave a small contribution. It is important to end the pilgrimage at St. Roch Chapel and find a four-leaf clover in the cemetery. This should result in a successful marriage before the year is out. One of the stops includes The Original National Shrine of St. Ann in Tremé-Lafitte.

THE LIVING STATIONS OF THE CROSS
St. Peter Claver Catholic Church Youth Ministry
1923 St. Philip Street - Tremé-Lafitte

A traditional event worthy of reflection, is the annual Living Stations of the Cross recreated by members of the St. Peter Claver Catholic Church Youth Ministry. It is always staged on the altar on Good Friday and is a moving tribute to The Passion of Jesus Christ.

"MAKING" THE NINE CHURCHES
Good Friday
St. John the Baptist Catholic Church
1139 Oretha Castle Haley Boulevard - Central City

THE HOLY SPIRIT

"And the Holy Spirit descended ... like a dove upon Him ..."
- Luke 3:22

ST. RITA OF CASCIA CATHOLIC CHURCH
2729 Lowerline Street - Marlyville-Fontainebleau
Entrance Tympanum

ST. MARY'S ASSUMPTION CHURCH
919 Josephine Street - Lower Garden District
Pulpit Canopy Detail

VIA CRUCIS
STATION VII

Jesus Falls the Second Time

ST. MARY'S ASSUMPTION CHURCH
919 Josephine Street - Lower Garden District

*" ... as the cross grows heavier and heavier
it becomes more difficult ... "*

Crescent City Saints: Religious Icons of New Orleans

"Which hope we have as an anchor of the soul, both sure and steadfast ..."
- Hebrews 6:19

THE VIRTUE OF HOPE
The Cathedral-Basilica of St. Louis King of France
Jackson Square - French Quarter

Of the Seven Virtues, three are considered theological. They include the familiar, Faith, Hope, and Charity. Hope is generally accompanied by an anchor, the traditional symbol of hope.

"Spes Unica" - Our Only Hope

AVE CRUX, SPES UNICA
Sacred Heart Catholic Church - 139 Canal Street - Mid-City

This architectural medallion depicts the cross with the anchors of hope. The Latin inscription comes from the motto, *Ave Crux, Spes Unica* - Hail to the Cross, our only Hope. It is thought to be a stanza from a 6th century Roman hymn and is a motto used by a number of religious institutions.

NORWEGIAN'S SEAMEN'S CHURCH
1772 Prytania Street - Lower Garden District

This anchor rests at the entrance of the Norwegian Seamen's Church as a symbol of an 'anchorage' for sailors visiting New Orleans. It also conveys the religious significance of the mariners' cross and anchor of hope.

THE SON OF THUNDER

SAINT JAMES MAJOR
St. James Major Catholic Church and School
3736 Gentilly Boulevard - Gentilly Terrace and Gardens

Saint James the Greater has a cockle hat, staff, and wears scallop shells. These are the traditional symbols of a pilgrim. He was one of the Twelve Apostles and the brother of John. The pilgrimage to the grave of St. James in Spain is known as *The Way of St. James* and is popular with Christians throughout the world. Part of the route follows the sea and pilgrims often pick up shells as souvenirs of their journey. Pilgrims are usually depicted with scallop shells on their hats, clothes, and pouches. Saint James is the patron of Spain.

THE JESUITS

"Ad Majorem Dei Gloriam" - For the Greater Glory of God

The earliest religious services were held in New Orleans by Jesuit missionaries. They arrived here with Iberville and Bienville with the sole purpose of establishing the Catholic Church for the conversion of Native Americans. The Jesuits were also responsible for introducing the cultivation of oranges and sugar cane to the colony.

THE JESUIT CREST
Chapel Of The North American Martyrs - Jesuit High School
S. Solomon and Palmyra Streets - Mid-City
Pediment Detail

The Jesuit crest includes the Sacred Monogram of Jesus Christ. This beautiful illustration of the official seal of the Society of Jesus contains the characters IHS in capitals. The cross rests on the crossbeam of the letter H. Iota, eta, and sigma are the first three letters in the Greek spelling of Jesus. The three converging nails represent the crucifixion.

EVENTS IN THE LIFE OF JESUS CHRIST

" ... Hail, thou who art full of grace; the Lord is with thee; Blessed art thou among women." **- Luke 1:28**

THE ANNUNCIATION
Saints Peter and Paul Catholic Church
In Situ - 2317 Burgundy Street - Faubourg Marigny - Closed 2001
Statue relocated to: Blessed Francis Xavier Seelos Parish

THE NATIVITY
Our Lady Star of the Sea Catholic Church
1835 St. Roch Avenue - Faubourg St. Roch

"The more you honor Me, the more I will bless you."

THE INFANT OF PRAGUE
Prager Tomb - Metairie Cemetery - Lakewood
Our Lady of Prompt Succor National Shrine - Audubon

The Infant of Prague is a popular depiction of the Christ Child. The image is believed to have originated as a 19-inch, wax-coated wooden figure that once belonged to St. Teresa of Ávila. The infant is traditionally shown wearing imperial regalia including the imperial crown and holding the globus cruciger, or cross-bearing orb. The orb is the sign of authority illustrating Christ's dominion over the world.

His right hand forms the gesture of the blessing or benediction. Two raised fingers represent the divine and human natures of Our Lord. The two bent fingers and thumb represent the Holy Trinity.

During the siege of Prague by the Swedish Army in 1639, the citizens prayed to this little statue day and night. When the army left the city, the Holy Infant was given credit for the miracle. This incident parallels a similar event in New Orleans when the statue of Our Lady of Prompt Succor was venerated for Jackson's victory at the Battle of New Orleans.

THE HOLY CHILD
Holy Child Jesus Academy
Convent of the Perpetual Adoration - Closed 2005
St. Maurice Avenue and Chartres Street - Lower Nine

Jesus holds a sheaf of wheat and grapes, symbols of the Eucharist. Wheat is also a symbol of a life fulfilled as well as immortality. A nearly identical statue of the Holy Child can be found at the entrance of Holy Name of Jesus Catholic Church on St. Charles Avenue. This photograph was taken several months after Hurricane Katrina. The building remains abandoned.

THE BAPTISM OF JESUS
Blessed Francis Xavier Seelos Parish Catholic Church
3053 Dauphine Street - Bywater

THE GOOD SHEPHERD
Notre Dame Seminary Campus
2901 S. Carrollton Avenue - Marlyville-Fontainebleau

JESUS AND THE SAMARITAN WOMAN AT JACOB'S WELL
Notre Dame Seminary Campus - May 1989
Original centerpiece of the Vatican Pavilion
1984 Louisiana World Exposition
Ivan Mestrovic - 1984

THE SACRED HEART OF JESUS
St. Anthony's Garden
Royal Street at Orleans - French Quarter

An inspirational and beloved feature of the French Quarter is the graceful white marble statue of *The Sacred Heart of Jesus* in St. Anthony's Garden. It was placed there in memory of New Orleans banker J. E. Merilh and his wife. In the early evening, a floodlight casts a towering shadow of the outstretched arms of Jesus onto the rear wall of the cathedral creating a stunning image. In 2005, a large tree fell during Hurricane Katrina detaching several fingers from the left hand of Jesus. Archbishop Alfred Hughes vowed to fix the damage when he felt that the city had fully recovered from the storm. In 2018, repairs began in time to celebrate the Tricentennial of New Orleans.

THE SACRED HEART OF JESUS
Sacred Heart Catholic Church - 139 Canal Street - Mid-City

JESUS CHRIST PANTOCRATOR
Holy Trinity Greek Orthodox Cathedral
1200 Robert E. Lee Boulevard - Lakeview
Laurence Manos - 2000

This is the icon of Jesus Christ Pantocrator or *Ruler of All*. He is surrounded by the angelic powers, looking down upon creation from the dome of the Greek Orthodox Cathedral. He holds the New Testament in His left hand. He makes the blessing gesture with His right hand, arranging His fingers in the shape of the Greek letters IC XC, the monogram of Jesus (**IHCOYC**) Christ (**XPICTOC**). The letters *omicron, omega,* and *nu,* surrounding Christ's head indicate, *the one who is*.

THE PASSION
Bisque Portrait - St. Patrick Cemetery #3 - Navarre

"ECCE HOMO" — Behold the Man
Blessed Francis Xavier Seelos Parish Catholic Church
3053 Dauphine Street - Bywater

THE CRUCIFIXION
**Saint Michael the Archangel Chapel Entrance
St. Roch Cemetery #2 - Campo Santo
St. Roch Avenue at N. Derbigny Street - Faubourg St. Roch**

This traditional Calvary grouping was sculpted in Carrara, Italy. It was imported by the Acme Marble & Granite Company and blessed on Good Friday, April 12, 1963.

In consideration of their gift, the cemetery administration has pledged to the donors that the services of Good Friday and All Saints terminate with the traditional sermon before this Calvary group.
- **Monument Inscription**

THE LAMENTATION
Blessed Francis Xavier Seelos Parish Catholic Church
3053 Dauphine Street - Bywater

ENTOMBED JESUS
St. Roch Cemetery #1 - Campo Santo
St. Roch at N. Derbigny Street - Faubourg St. Roch

This dramatic presentation of *Entombed Jesus* is usually displayed in churches on Good Friday and Holy Saturday to remind us of His presence in the tomb. Traditionally removed from sight by Easter morning, this example is always on display in a grotto-like setting beneath the main altar of the Chapel of St. Roch at The National Shrine of St. Roch.

"The last enemy that shall be destroyed is death." - **1 Corinthians 15:26**

THE RESURRECTION
St. Paul Lutheran Church
Port & Burgundy Streets - Faubourg Marigny
Frederick Wilhelm Wehle - 1892

*"His face shown like the sun,
And His clothes became as white as the light."*
- Matthew 17:2

**THE TRANSFIGURATION
St. Stephen Catholic Church
1025 Napoleon Avenue - Touro**

*"When He had led them out to the vicinity of Bethany,
he lifted up His hands and blessed them.
While He was blessing them,
He left them and was taken up into heaven."*
- Luke 25:50-51

THE ASCENSION
Immaculate Conception Church
130 Baronne Street - Central Business District

The traditional Stations of the Cross include meditations on 14 events in The Passion of Christ. The stained glass windows at Immaculate Conception Church depict four additional events creating a more scripturally accurate version of The Passion. The customary 14 stations are preceded by the Agony of Jesus and the Crown of Thorns, and followed by the Resurrection and the Ascension. The Delivery of The Keys to St. Peter, from Matthew 16:18, is also depicted in this window.

THE MOST HOLY SAVIOR
Santissimo Salvatore Patron of Cefalù
The Società Italiana di Mutua Beneficenza Cefalùtana
St. Louis Cemetery #3 - Esplanade Ridge

The Società Cefalùtana was founded in New Orleans in 1887. It was created to assist immigrants from Cefalù, Sicily, in times of illness, death, financial need, and cultural assimilation. The SS in the inscription stands for Santissimo or *Most Holy* Savior.

VIA CRUCIS
STATION VIII

Jesus Meets the Women of Jerusalem

THE CATHEDRAL-BASILICA OF ST. LOUIS KING OF FRANCE
Jackson Square - French Quarter

" ... As you pass by, you see they are sad ... "

MAID OF ORLÉANS

SAINT JOAN OF ARC
**New Place De France - Decatur and St. Philip - French Quarter
Emmanuel Fremiet - Place des Pyramids - Paris
Copy Presented to New Orleans: April 18, 1964**

The French peasant, Joan of Arc, received a vision from the Archangel Michael to assist in the fight to recover France from English domination. She gained prominence after the victory at the siege of Orléans. Soon thereafter, she was captured by the English and burned at the stake when she was only 19 years old. Pope Callixtus III declared her innocent and made her a martyr. St. Joan of Arc is the patron of soldiers, prisoners, and the Women's Army Corps.

SAINT JOAN OF ARC MAUSOLEUM
St. Roch Cemetery #1 - Campo Santo
St. Roch at N. Derbigny Street - Faubourg St. Roch

SAINT JOAN OF ARC CATHOLIC CHURCH
8321 Burthe Street - Riverbend
Entrance Tympanum

"A Voice Crying Aloud In The Wilderness"

SAINT JOHN THE BAPTIST
St. John the Baptist Catholic Church
1139 Oretha Castle Haley Boulevard - Central City

Saint John the Baptist is wearing loin coverings made of camel hair pelts and a leather belt and pouch from which he ate insects and wild honey. These are symbolic of his ascetic life spent in the wilderness, as is the reed cross he carries. He is announcing the coming of Christ and proclaiming baptism for the forgiveness of sins.

SAINT JOHN'S EVE - June 23, 2014
The Magnolia Bridge - Bayou St. John

June 23 is an important day for practitioners of Voodoo because of the summer solstice's general alignment with the Feast of St. John the Baptist. The Voodoo priestess of New Orleans, Marie Laveau, held her secret rituals at the *Wishing Spot* along the banks of Bayou St. John near Lake Pontchartrain on St. John's Eve. A similar tradition is still observed today at the Magnolia Bridge. Celebrants, dressed in white, engage in a head cleansing ceremony, or lave tet. Offerings to Laveau include food, wine, hair ribbons, rosaries, candles, and flowers.

"Totus Tuus" - Totally Yours

SANCTUS JOANNES PAULUS II
St. Patrick Mausoleum - St. Patrick Cemetery #3
City Park Avenue at Virginia Street - Navarre

POPE JOHN PAUL II
Papal Visit to New Orleans - September 11-13, 1987

PLACE JOHN PAUL II
The Cathedral-Basilica of St. Louis King of France
Place John Paul II - 700 Chartres Street - French Quarter

Pope John Paul's visit to New Orleans included prayers at the St. Louis Cathedral, a French Quarter parade, and a youth rally at the Superdome. A late afternoon outdoor mass brought the Pope to the UNO campus in sweltering summer heat. Thunderstorms began to gather, along with an enormous crowd, giving way to a torrential downpour. Local lore has it that as soon as the Popemobile entered the grounds the rain stopped and the service went on as planned. The newspaper reported that vendors were offering worshippers a chance to cool down by selling frozen *Popesicles*. As a permanent memorial of John Paul's visit to New Orleans, one block of Chartres, in front the Cathedral, was renamed La Place Jean-Paul Deux.

"Go To Joseph"

SAINT JOSEPH
St. Joseph Church - 1802 Tulane Avenue - Tulane-Gravier
Original location: Hotel Dieu - 2021 Perdido Street
Daprato Statuary Company - 1891

SAINT JOSEPH
St. Joseph Academy and Convent Detail
Ursulines at Galvez Street - Tremé-Lafitte

As a member of the Holy Family, Saint Joseph has a unique position along with the Virgin Mother just below the Holy Trinity and above all other saints and angels. Joseph's traditional depiction as a bearded, older man visually reinforces the celibacy of the Holy Mother. He is the patron of families, immigrants, social justice, and real estate. The advice given to anyone who wants favor with the Holy Family is to, *"Go to Joseph."*

Due to the influx of Sicilian immigrants in the 1850s, St. Joseph became a highly venerated saint in the City of New Orleans. His feast day, March 19, centers around a season of multicultural events throughout the city. Celebrations largely coincide with Saint Patrick's Day festivities featuring neighborhood parades, ethnic feasting, marching clubs, public and private St. Joseph's Altars, as well as appearances by the Mardi Gras Indians.

Saint Teresa of Ávila often prayed to Saint Joseph to help her locate suitable land for Christian converts. He became known as the patron of property owners. There is a belief that burying a statue of St. Joseph on your property will help sell your house. This tradition has continued over the years and New Orleans homeowners choose to bury their statue of St. Joseph upside down in hopes of a speedy sale. It seems that in this awkward position, St. Joseph is better motivated to act quickly.

The Mardi Gras Indians make one of their traditional appearances on the Sunday closest to St. Joseph's Day known as Super Sunday. They can generally be found along Bayou St. John, A. L. Davis Park in Central City, and Hunter's Field in the Seventh Ward. They appear again on St. Joseph's Night with a neighborhood party and march through Central City. The festivities begin at Washington Avenue and LaSalle Street.

THE JOSEPHITES

The Saint Joseph Society of the Sacred Heart is a congregation of priests and brothers whose mission is to serve the African American community.

SAINT JOSEPH WITH YOUNG JESUS
An African American Devotion
Catholic Cultural Heritage Center
Ursuline Convent - French Quarter
Original location: Holy Ghost Parish - New Orleans

SAINT JOSEPH'S ALTAR
Immaculate Conception Church
130 Baronne Street - Central Business District

Legend has it that a severe drought occurred in Sicily during the Middle Ages. Prayers to their patron, Saint Joseph, resulted in rain, saving the faithful from starvation. As a result, the people prepared a large feast in his honor and continue to do so today. The tradition spread and is now an important part of the religious landscape of New Orleans. Saint Joseph's Altars can be found in many public and private locations throughout the city leading up to March 19.

It is believed that the fava, or lucky bean, produced the crop that prevented the famine and has become a significant feature of the Saint Joseph's Altar tradition. The altar is constructed in three layers which represent the Holy Trinity. Decorations include a statue of St. Joseph, candles, cakes, cookies, flowers, wine, and assorted meatless dishes. Fish is popular, as it was a Christian symbol during persecution. Since Joseph was a carpenter, the bread crumbs used in cooking represent sawdust. Saint Joseph Bread is baked in shapes resembling saws and hammers. Much attention is given to these altars and they are very personal works of art. Each one has a special meaning to the family for favors granted or cures received. The altars are blessed on March 18, often in the afternoon. Visitors are given a small bag containing a fava bean, cookies, and a prayer card. Leftovers are distributed to the poor.

THE INTERNATIONAL SHRINE OF ST. JUDE

SAINT JUDE THADDEUS
Our Lady of Guadalupe Church - Peace Garden
411 N. Rampart Street - Tremé

Our Lady of Guadalupe Church is home to The International Shrine of Saint Jude. Jude Thaddeus was one of the Twelve Apostles of Jesus. He is holding a large club symbolizing his martyrdom in Persia. The flame on his head is evidence of his presence at the Pentecost. Jude also carries an icon of the Image of Edessa, the holy relic of cloth on which the miraculous image of Christ appeared. The shrine has become the focus of daily devotion and prayer in New Orleans. This 17-foot image is believed to be the largest in the world. The solemn St. Jude Novena is held every three months for those in desperate situations. St. Jude is the patron of impossible causes.

SAINT JEANNE JUGAN L.S.P.
Foundress - Little Sisters of the Poor
St. Louis Cemetery #3 - Esplanade Ridge

Saint Jugan is the patron of the impoverished and the elderly. She was born in France in 1792, and dedicated her life to caring for senior citizens. She began by taking elderly women into her home and soon began renting rooms for dozens of destitute and sick people. She founded the Little Sisters of the Poor, eventually expanding her efforts throughout the world. Jugan was canonized as recently as 2009.

Dedicated to the People of New Orleans who enabled her daughters to serve the aged poor of the city for 137 years through their prayers and their unfailing collaboration.

- Monument Inscription

SAINT LEO THE GREAT
St. Leo The Great Catholic Church
St. Raymond and St. Leo The Great Catholic Parishes
2916 Paris Avenue - Seventh Ward

Pope Leo I was a Doctor of the Church, well-versed in scripture and theology. He was an eloquent preacher and writer. Leo spoke about basic human dignity and equality. *"The saint, the sinner and the unbeliever are all equal as sinners. None is excluded in the call to happiness."* He is remembered as the Pope who successfully negotiated with Attila the Hun.

VIA CRUCIS
STATION IX
Jesus Falls the Third Time

OUR LADY OF GUADALUPE
411 N. Rampart Street - Tremé

*" ... for the third time
the heavy cross bowed Thee to the earth ... "*

SAINT LOUIS IX - KING OF FRANCE
The Cathedral-Basilica of St. Louis King of France
Jackson Square - French Quarter

SAINT LOUIS IX - KING OF FRANCE
Saint Augustine Church
Governor Nicholls and Henriette Delille Streets - Tremé

Louis IX was a devout Catholic and the only French king ever canonized by the Church. He technically became King of France at the age of 12 and grew to imagine his mission as the, *lieutenant of God on Earth*. Even as a child, he was a champion of the poor, feeding hundreds who ate with him at the palace. He is seen here wearing his crown and holding a scepter which is topped with a fleur-de-lis. He is also holding the relic of the original Crown of Thorns which was given to him by Baldwin II, the Latin Emperor of Constantinople in 1238. St. Louis is the patron of France, hairdressers, and grooms.

SAINT IGNATIUS OF LOYOLA
Thomas Hall - Loyola University
6363 St. Charles Avenue - Audubon
A Gift from Mr. and Mrs. John P. Laborde

St. Ignatius Loyola 1491-1556 - Founder of the Jesuits And Patron of the University - Pray for Us
  - Monument Inscription

On the Loyola campus, Saint Ignatius is popularly known as *Iggy*. His statue is often attired in t-shirts or other garments reflecting the time of year or current event. He has been seen in Mardi Gras costumes and sports uniforms, often to the dismay of university officials.

SAINT IGNATIUS OF LOYOLA
Marquette Hall Entrance - Loyola University
6363 St. Charles Avenue - Audubon
The Pan American Club - 1950

Íñigo López de Loyola was wounded in the Battle of Pamplona and experienced a religious conversion during his recovery. He abandoned the military and followed the example of various spiritual leaders including St. Francis of Assisi. He founded the Society of Jesus, or the Jesuits. The society serves the pope as missionaries. Saint Ignatius of Loyola is the patron of Loyola University, Catholic soldiers, educators, as well as various towns and cities.

This statue, based on a painting by Miguel Cabrera, depicts Ignatius standing over the powerful fallen angel, Lucifer. It is symbolic of the constant battle between good and evil. Ignatius is holding a book with the inscription, *Ad majorem Dei gloriam*, which is the Latin motto of the Jesuits. The book represents the many religious writings credited to Ignatius. The English translation is, *For the Greater Glory of God.*

The abbreviation AMDG is often found on buildings and statues associated with the Society of Jesus. A longer version of the phrase, *Ad majorem Dei gloriam inque hominum salute*, means, *For the Greater Glory of God and Salvation of Man.*

SANTA LUCIA

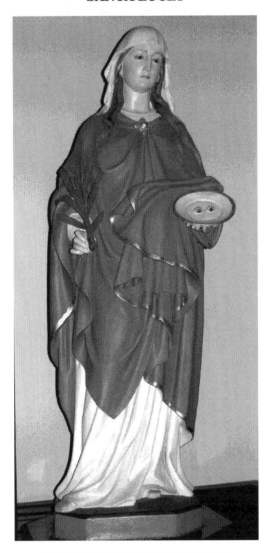

SAINT LUCY OF SYRACUSE
St. John the Baptist Church
1139 Oretha Castle Haley Boulevard - Central City

Lucia of Syracuse holds a palm frond indicating that she was a Christian martyr who achieved victory over evil. Legend has it that her martyrdom included the gouging of her eyes, therefore she is depicted holding a golden dish with two eyes. She is the patron of the blind. La Societa de Santa Lucia di New Orleans holds its annual December mass at St. John the Baptist Church in Central City for those who live with eye disorders.

VIRGIN OF THE CLIFF

MADONNA DEL BALZO
Società Italiana Di Mutua Beneficenza
Madonna Del Monte Triona Da Bisacquino
Metairie Cemetery - Section 95 - Lakewood

This remarkable image of the Madonna Del Balzo, the *Virgin of the Cliff*, surmounts this Italian society tomb in Metairie Cemetery. The original Sanctuary of Madonna del Balzo rests on a steep cliff on Mount Triona in Sicily, near the city of Bisacquino. In 1664, two children climbed the mountain to play games and gamble. The loser threw a stone against a rock containing the image of the Virgin. When her forehead began to bleed, the youngster fainted. A crowd climbed the mountain and the child's mother asked the Virgin to have mercy on her son. The child woke up and began cheering the Virgin. This was interpreted as a miracle and a sanctuary to the Madonna was erected.

THE PEARL OF SCOTLAND

SAINT MARGARET OF SCOTLAND AND DAVID
St. Margaret's Daughters' Home - Closed 2005
In Situ - 500 Tricou Street - Holy Cross

Margaret was recognized for her purity, charity work, and devotion to her Church. She is holding her treasured book of the Gospels which was adorned with jewels. Margaret was a leader in Scotland's religious, artistic, and educational reformation. She gave special attention to her youngest son, David, teaching him to become an honest and holy ruler. He became David I, King of Scotland.

This photograph of the statue of St. Margaret of Scotland was taken a few months following Hurricane Katrina which destroyed the Home on Tricou Street. The statue, which survived the hurricane, was later relocated to St. Claude Avenue where it was destroyed by vandals in 2013. The Home reopened as St. Margaret's at Mercy at 3525 Bienville Street in the same block as the old Mercy Hospital in Mid-City.

"Fear not my children for I shall never abandon you."

MARIA S. S. DEL SOCCORSO SCIACCA
Società Italiana Di Mutua Beneficenza
Metairie Cemetery - Section 86 - Lakewood

This magnificent sculpture surmounts an Italian society tomb in Metairie Cemetery. Madonna Del Soccorso, *Our Lady of Help*, is patron of the town of Sciacca, Italy. She appeared in Sciacca in response to the plight of a six-year-old boy who was taken from his mother by the devil. The Blessed Mother appeared in a beautiful gold and white robe. She knocked the devil to the ground with one swing of a club and stood on top of him. Instead of running to his mother, the boy ran to Maria and hid under her cape. The girl, also looking out from under the cape, represents another miracle in Sciacca. This paralyzed 13-year-old followed Maria's instructions to touch her belt so she could walk again. After rescuing Sciacca from the plague of 1626, she was offered the keys to the city. If you look closely at the statue, you can see them hanging from her belt. The SS in the tomb inscription stands for Santissima or *Most Holy*.

PÉRE JACQUES MARQUETTE S.J.
**Marquette Hall Entrance - Loyola University
6363 St. Charles Avenue - Audubon**

    Religion was the reason that Jacques Marquette become an explorer. He joined the Society of Jesus when he was 17 and eventually became a Jesuit missionary. Pére Marquette established several missions for the Native Americans. In 1673, he and his friend, Louis Joliet, set out on their famous exploration of the Mississippi River. This statue in honor of Marquette stands at the main entrance of Marquette Hall on the Loyola University campus. Note the crucifix tucked into his sash. The Pére Marquette office building at 817 Common Street is now the Renaissance New Orleans Pére Marquette Hotel.

*"They are lost souls and must be brought back
into the Bosom of my Son,
otherwise this would break His heart."*
- **Your Beloved Mother**

MARY, QUEEN OF POOR SOULS
The Cathedral-Basilica of St. Louis King of France
Jackson Square - French Quarter

HAIL O MARY, MOTHER OF MERCY
Loyola University - 2038 Calhoun Street - Audubon

This is a beautiful, yet unusual textured stone sculpture of Mary and the Christ Child. Mary wears a long robe and is seated on the throne of heaven holding the infant Jesus in her lap. She wears the crown of her coronation and holds a metal cross in her right hand. Jesus sits in the center of Mary's lap holding a metal candle in his left hand and an orb in his right. A halo is positioned just behind his head.

MATER DOLOROSA

There are three traditional representations of Our Lady of Sorrow found in religious art and sculpture. One depiction is the Mater Dolorosa, shown here. The other two examples include the Pietà and the Stabat Mater. The familiar Pietà shows the Virgin Mary cradling the body of Jesus. The Stabat Mater Dolorosa - *the sorrowful mother stood* - is generally found in the traditional Crucifixion scene where Mary is always shown standing on the right hand side of Jesus.

MATER DOLOROSA
Blessed Francis Xavier Seelos Parish Catholic Church
3053 Dauphine Street - Bywater

"Et Cecidit Sors Super Matthiam"
And the Lot Fell upon Matthias

SAINT MATTHIAS
St. Matthias Catholic Church
4230 South Broad Street - Broadmoor

"And they gave forth their lots; and the lot fell upon Matthias; and he was numbered with the eleven apostles." - **Acts 1:26**

Saint Matthias was chosen by the Apostles to replace Judas Iscariot following the betrayal. He is generally depicted holding an executioner's axe, the symbol of his martyrdom.

SAINT MATTHIAS
St. Matthias Catholic School
Gen. Taylor and S. Dorgenois Streets - Broadmoor
School Pediment Detail - 1928

Saint Matthias's Day, February 24, is said to be the luckiest day of the year. Since the lot fell upon Matthias to replace Judas, it is considered to be a good day to buy a lottery ticket. Matthias is the patron of carpenters and tailors. St. Matthias Church is now home to the Blessed Trinity Parish.

Crescent City Saints: Religious Icons of New Orleans

VIA CRUCIS
STATION X

Jesus' Clothes are Taken Away

ST. PATRICK CEMETERY #1
Canal Street and City Park Avenue - Mid-City

"... stripped of Thy garments and drenched with gall ..."

MAUNDY THURSDAY

THE LAST SUPPER
Blessed Francis Xavier Seelos Parish Catholic Church
Main Altar Detail - 3053 Dauphine Street - Bywater

The term Maundy Thursday refers to the *mandatum* Christ gave to His followers at the Last Supper as recorded in John 13:34. In New Orleans, Maundy Thursday has its own unique traditions and, as with the Last Supper, it involves food. Every year, Chef Leah Chase, of Dookie Chase Restaurant, hosts an annual lunch featuring her Creole specialty, *gumbo z'herbes*. The reference is a contraction of the term *gumbo aux herbs* or gumbo with greens. The number of greens used in the traditional recipe is always an odd number. In Leah's case, she uses nine different herbs and claims that to be the number of new friends you will make during the next year. Nine is also important in New Orleans as it is the number of churches one traditionally visits on Good Friday.

HOLY TRINITY GREEK ORTHODOX CATHEDRAL
1200 Robert E. Lee Boulevard - Lakeview

SAINT MICHAEL THE ARCHANGEL
Blessed Francis Xavier Seelos Parish Catholic Church
3053 Dauphine Street - Bywater
Original Location: Sts. Peter & Paul Catholic Church - Marigny

"Quis ut Deus? Serviam!"
Who is like God? I will serve!

The Archangel Michael swore his allegiance to God the Father Almighty and proved his loyalty by opposing the rebellious angels led by Lucifer. Revelation 12:7 describes the war in heaven where the angelic warrior Michael prevails in the epic battle between good and evil. In his fall from heaven, Lucifer attempts to take Michael down with him. God intervenes and saves His servant Michael allowing Lucifer to, *"fall like lightning from heaven."*

> *"The Holy Church venerates thee as its Guardian and Patron; and it glories in the fact that thou art its Defender against the wicked powers of Earth and Hell."*
> **- Pope Leo XIII**

He is often depicted in full armor, with a helmet and sword, carrying a shield bearing the definition of his name, *Quis ut Deus*. He stands victorious over Satan who is sometimes portrayed as a dragon. Saint Michael is the patron of police departments due to his association with the struggle of good over evil.

THE CHAPEL OF SAINT MICHAEL THE ARCHANGEL
St. Roch Cemetery #2 - Campo Santo
St. Roch at N. Derbigny Street - Faubourg St. Roch

NOAH'S ARK
Audubon Park & Zoological Garden
6500 Magazine Street - Audubon
Hans Mengelsdorf - 1939

THE NORTH AMERICAN MARTYRS
Chapel Of The North American Martyrs - Jesuit High School
S. Solomon and Palmyra Streets - Mid-City

This pediment detail depicts three of the eight Jesuit missionaries who sacrificed their lives while teaching and spreading the Gospel throughout North America. At the center is Saint Isaac Jogues who is joined by his companions, Saint René Goupil and Saint Juan de la Lande. All three were canonized in 1930.

PATRONESS OF CUBA

OUR LADY OF CHARITY
Nuestra Señora De La Caridad Del Cobre
St. Anthony Of Padua Church
4640 Canal Street - Mid-City

When the de Hoyos brothers and the young slave, Juan Moreno, set to sea in the Bay of Nipe, they had no concept of the spiritual fate that awaited them. The Cuban waters began to toss their canoe as a sudden storm arose. Juan, the young slave boy, was wearing a medal bearing the image of the Virgin Mary. When the three began to pray and the seas calmed, they spotted an object floating in the distance. It turned out to be a small statue of the Holy Mother holding Jesus in her left arm and a small gold cross in her right hand. The Child Jesus forms the sign of the blessing with His right hand and holds a golden globe in His left. A message attached to the statue read: *"Yo Soy la Virgen de la Caridad,"* - I am the Virgin of Charity. They brought the 16-inch statue back to town eventually moving it to El Cobre, Cuba, where a beautiful shrine stands today in her honor. She is known as *Nuestra Señora de la Caridad del Cobre* - Our Lady of Charity of El Cobre. Our Lady of Charity is the Patroness of Cuba.

NOSSA SENHORA DE FÁTIMA

OUR LADY OF FÁTIMA
St. Clare's Monastery Garden
720 Henry Clay Avenue - Audubon

Lúcia Santos and her cousins Jacinta and Francisco Marto were three shepherd children who are said to have witnessed the Marian apparitions at Fátima, Portugal. The apparitions occurred on the thirteenth day of six consecutive months in 1917. Lúcia described the Lady as, *"brighter than the sun, shedding rays of light."* The visits by Mary were preceded in 1916, by the appearance of an angel who taught the children special prayers and how to offer sacrifices. Our Lady also confided three secrets to the children, known as the Three Secrets of Fátima. At one point, the children were actually jailed and threatened to reveal the secrets. The first secret was a vision of hell. The second involved a prediction referring to World War I. The controversial third secret was revealed 83 years later, involving the persecution of Christians and the assassination of the pope. At her final appearance on October 13, 1917, the *Miracle of the Sun* was witnessed by an estimated 70,000 people. The sun is said to have appeared as a silver disk. It eventually changed colors and began to rotate like a wheel.

The Miracle of Our Lady of Fátima is one of the greatest religious events celebrated in sculpture and art throughout the City of New Orleans. The traditional setting of the three shepherd children witnessing the vision of Our Lady can be found in convent gardens and several churches.

OUR LADY OF FÁTIMA
Holy Name of Jesus Church - Mary Side Altar Detail
6367 St. Charles Avenue - Audubon

OUR LADY OF FÁTIMA
The Archbishop's Residence - Rear Garden
7900 Walmsley Avenue - Marlyville-Fontainebleau

PATRONESS OF THE AMERICAS

OUR LADY OF GUADALUPE
Our Lady of Guadalupe (Old Mortuary Chapel)
411 N. Rampart Street - Tremé

The miraculous image of the Virgin of Guadalupe appeared on the fabric of Juan Diego's cloak following the Marian Appearance of 1531, near Mexico City. She spoke to him in Nahuatl, the language of the Aztecs, requesting that a church be built at the site of her appearance.

The Chapel of St. Anthony, the Old Mortuary Chapel in New Orleans, eventually became known as Our Lady of Guadalupe Church in order to serve the Spanish speaking population of New Orleans. Is it also the official church of the New Orleans Police and Fire Departments.

"... and upon her head a crown of twelve stars."
- Revelation 12:12

OUR LADY OF THE IMMACULATE CONCEPTION
Immaculate Conception Church
130 Baronne Street - Central Business District

The Immaculate Conception does not refer to the Virgin birth of Jesus. It describes Mary's personal conception in her mother's womb. God filled Mary with grace and kept her apart from original sin in anticipation of the virtues of Jesus.

This solid marble statue was carved in France and stands in a delicately lighted niche high above the main altar. The arc of twelve lights represent the twelve stars of Revelation.

OUR LADY OF LA VANG
Our Lady of La Vang Catholic Church
6054 Vermillion Boulevard - St. Anthony

In the early part of the 19th century, Our Lady appeared to a large group of persecuted Vietnamese Catholics hiding in the forests of La Vang in Central Vietnam. She was holding Jesus in her arms and accompanied by two angels. She encouraged and comforted the hungry and sick, presenting herself as Mary, The Mother of God.

The Shrine to Our Lady of La Vang in New Orleans is a interesting mixture of Vietnamese architecture and Catholic iconography located in the Gentilly neighborhood of St. Anthony.

OUR LADY OF LOURDES GROTTO
Saint Bernadette and The Immaculate Conception
St. Leo The Great Catholic Church
St. Raymond and St. Leo The Great Catholic Parishes
2916 Paris Avenue - Seventh Ward

This small grotto in the side yard of St. Leo the Great Catholic Church, depicts one of 18 appearances of Our Lady to the young peasant girl near Lourdes, France, in 1858. When Bernadette Soubirous encountered the vision, she asked, *"Who are you?"* Our Lady replied, *"I am the Immaculate Conception."*

Bernadette eventually joined the Sisters of Charity. She died on April 16, 1879, at the age of 35. Because her body appeared to be incorruptible, she was canonized on December 8, 1933. St. Bernadette is the patron of bodily illnesses, shepherds, the poor, and people who are ridiculed for their faith.

NATIONAL SHRINE OF OUR LADY OF PROMPT SUCCOR
Patroness of New Orleans and Louisiana

OUR LADY OF PROMPT SUCCOR
The National Shrine Of Our Lady Of Prompt Succor
2701 State Street - Audubon

In 1810, the statue of Our Lady was brought from France to the Ursuline Convent in the French Quarter. On the eve of the Battle of New Orleans, the Ursulines and citizens prayed before the statue of the Virgin throughout the night. Our Lady's veneration has been celebrated with the Mass of Thanksgiving on the 8th of January every year since Jackson's victory over the British in 1815. This tradition continues at The National Shrine of Our Lady of Prompt Succor on the Ursuline College campus on State Street.

"Mariae Victrici" – **To Mary the Victorious**

"THE SWEETHEART STATUE"

"Our Lady of Prompt Succor, we are lost unless you hasten to our aid."
- Mother St. Michel

OUR LADY OF PROMPT SUCCOR
The National Shrine Of Our Lady Of Prompt Succor
2701 State Street - Audubon

    This small plaster statue of Our Lady of Prompt Succor is just barely twelve inches tall. One of the Ursuline Sisters brought the icon from France in the 18th century. According to local folklore, this diminutive statue was placed in the window of the Ursuline Convent on Chartres Street during a French Quarter fire. The intercession of Our Lady was credited with sparing the destruction of the convent. The name *Sweetheart* comes from Mother St. Benoit's exclamation when she was told of the intervention of Our Lady - *"Oh, She's a Sweetheart."*
    This little statue is difficult to locate without help. It can be found in a small prayer room at the base of the bell tower protected by a glass case.

OUR LADY OF THE ROSARY
Our Lady of the Rosary Catholic Church
3368 Esplanade Avenue - Esplanade Ridge
Entrance Tympanum

This marble bas-relief sculpture shows Mary handing the rosary to Saint Dominic and the Child Jesus handing the rosary to St. Catherine of Siena.

OUR LADY OF THE SACRED HEART
Our Lady of the Sacred Heart Catholic Church
Our Lady of the Sacred Heart-St. Boniface Parish - Closed
1720 St. Bernard Avenue - Seventh Ward

"Therefore the Lord himself shall give you a sign; Behold, a virgin shall conceive, and bear a Son, and shall call His name Immanuel." - **Isaiah 7:14**

OUR LADY OF THE SIGN
Holy Trinity Greek Orthodox Cathedral
1200 Robert E. Lee Boulevard - Lakeview
Platytéra Iconography by Laurence Manos - 1987

Traditional icons of Our Lady of the Sign depict the Virgin Mary with the Child Jesus inside a round aureole on her breast representing the womb. This Greek interpretation shows Jesus seated on her right knee. In both cases, the image represents The Christ Child at the moment of conception in the womb. He is not depicted as a fetus but with the face of an adult. He is certainly the Son of God, divine and human. He is vested in white and gold robes suggesting His heavenly glory. The Child holds a scroll containing the Gospel, symbolic of His role as teacher. His other hand forms the sign of the blessing.

This particular icon is also referred to as the Platytéra. By holding the Creator of the Universe in her womb Mary has become *Platytéra ton ouranon*, which means, *more spacious than the heavens*. This is written in the space surrounding her image. Mary faces the viewer with her left hand extended in prayer. The letters MP ΘY above Mary's halo is an abbreviation for **MHTHP ΘEOY** - *Mother of God*. This image can be found inside the half-dome, or apse, above the Holy Table.

STELLA MARIS

OUR LADY, STAR OF THE SEA
Our Lady Star of the Sea Catholic Church
1835 St. Roch Avenue - Faubourg St. Roch

One of the oldest titles for the Virgin Mary is appropriate in a port city like New Orleans. She is patroness to Catholic missions to seafarers, and protector of those who make their living in the shipping industry. Stella Maris is also known as Polaris, the guiding star, used in navigation for centuries. Our Lady is our *steering star* which we follow on our way to find Christ.

OUR LADY OF THE WAY
Maria S. S. Odigitria Di Piana Dei Greci
Società Italiana Di Mutua Beneficenza

The Odigitria - *Hodegetria* - is an iconographic depiction of the Virgin Mary presenting the Christ Child to the world as the source of salvation. Hodegetria means *She Who Shows the Way*. She is the *Protettrice*, or guardian, of the city of Piana Dei Greci. The city is located in the province of Palermo, Sicily. It was founded in 1488, by a group of Albanian refugees who belonged to the Greek Orthodox Church. This intricate sculpture depicts two Albanian men dressed in traditional long red linen robes carrying the icon through the streets and town square during religious holidays. In 1941, the city was renamed, Piana degli Albanesi.

This icon, dated September 2, 1931, is the centerpiece of an imposing marble sanctuary honoring the members of this particular New Orleans Italian society. It is believed that the face of Mary used in the original Hodegetria icons were based on a painting by the Apostle Luke. The elaborate metal and ceramic details of this three dimensional depiction make this a truly inspirational and sacred work of art.

OUR MOTHER OF PERPETUAL HELP
2523 Prytania Street - Garden District

This beautifully detailed statue of Our Mother of Perpetual Help stands in a classical garden setting at the corner of Prytania and Third Streets. This was the former site of Our Mother of Perpetual Help Chapel which closed in the late 1990s. The adjoining mansion was once owned by Anne Rice and became the setting for several of her novels.

VIA CRUCIS
STATION XI

Jesus is Nailed to the Cross

HOLY NAME OF JESUS CATHOLIC CHURCH
6367 St. Charles Avenue - Audubon

" ... when the cruel nails pierced Thy tender hands..."

"O holy youth, come back to Erin and walk once more amongst us."

St. Patrick was not Irish. He was born in Scotland and captured by Irish marauders when he was in his teens. He was enslaved in Ireland for six years tending to the flocks of his captors. This experience lead him to a deeper relationship with God resulting in his conversion to Christianity. After escaping, he returned to his family and continued his religious studies. As the result of a vision, St. Patrick later returned to Ireland as a Christian missionary.

Because the three distinct leaves come together to form a whole, He used the Irish symbol of the shamrock to illustrate the concept of the Holy Trinity. St. Patrick wears a mitre and holds his celebrated golden crozier. It is supposed to be the *Bachal Isu* or the actual Staff of Jesus. If you look closely at the feet of St. Patrick, he is depicted standing next to a nest of snakes. Legend has it that he chased all of the snakes out of Ireland. Since there never were any snakes in Ireland, this story is most likely symbolic of his victories over paganism.

St. Patrick was never actually canonized by a pope but is venerated by the Christian Church as a saint in heaven. St. Patrick's Day is March 17, the date of his death.

St. Patrick is venerated by St. Patrick's Church, St. Patrick Cemeteries, and St. Patrick Street. On St. Patrick's Day weekend, New Orleans comes alive with neighborhood parades and Irish marching clubs handing out cabbages and kisses. There is also the traditional Irish Channel street party at Parasol's Bar at Constance and Third Streets.

APOSTLE OF IRELAND

SAINT PATRICK
St. Patrick Cemetery #3 - City Park Avenue - Navarre

Crescent City Saints: Religious Icons of New Orleans

APOSTLE, PREACHER, AND MARTYR

SAINT PETER
Immaculate Conception Church
130 Baronne Street - Central Business District

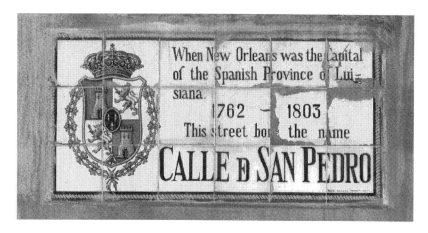

"... thou art Peter, and upon this rock I will build my church ... "
- Matthew 16:18

Simon Peter was one of the Twelve Apostles of Jesus Christ and brother of Andrew. Both were fishermen chosen by Christ to become disciples. According to traditional accounts, Peter was crucified in Rome. He chose to be hung on the cross upside down as he felt unworthy to die in the same manner as Jesus.

This statue of St. Peter is a faithful copy of the bronze statue from St. Peter's Basilica in Rome. It is a tradition for pilgrims to rub or kiss the right foot of St. Peter while saying a short prayer. You can see how the right foot is worn from the constant attention. The original Rome statue is thought to be the work of Arnolfo di Cambio. It depicts St. Peter, the first pope, giving the blessing and holding the Keys to the Kingdom. Visitors at Immaculate Conception Church leave their own keys at the feet of St. Peter as a sign of veneration.

He is the patron of bakers, locksmiths, masons, and fishermen.

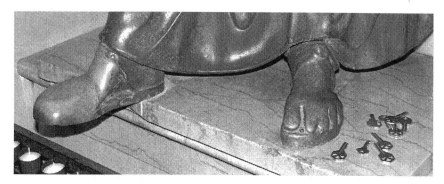

SAINT PETER STATUE DETAIL
Immaculate Conception Church
130 Baronne Street - Central Business District

THE PIETÀ

METAIRIE CEMETERY
Edith Allen Clark Tomb - Section 114 - Lakewood
Felix Weihs de Weldon - Sculptor

This bas-relief, gilded bronze medallion is 54 inches in diameter and depicts the traditional image of the Blessed Mother mourning the death of her Son, Jesus Christ. A host of cherubs populate the background.

SAINTS PETER AND PAUL CATHOLIC CHURCH
In Situ - 2317 Burgundy Street - Faubourg Marigny - Closed 2001
Relocated to: Blessed Francis Xavier Seelos Parish - Bywater

A PELICAN IN HER PIETY

LOUISIANA STATE SEAL
The National Eucharistic Congress - 1938
Our Lady of Guadalupe (The Old Mortuary Chapel)
Exterior Detail - 411 N. Rampart Street - Tremé

This stylized version of the Louisiana state seal, merged with the symbols of the Eucharist, was designed for the National Eucharistic Congress held in New Orleans in 1938. The official state seal depicts a mother Brown Pelican, the state bird, in the act of vulning. She is surrounded by three chicks and appears to be tearing at her flesh in order to feed her young. This is an ageless myth perpetuated by heraldic tradition. Pelicans only appear to be stabbing themselves in the chest as they attempt to pry food from their pouches to feed their young. However, the official symbol on the Louisiana state flag does include three drops of blood. This image suggests the generosity of Christ. The drops of blood, of course, represent the Holy Trinity.

Crescent City Saints: Religious Icons of New Orleans

There are illustrations of *A Pelican In Her Piety* in many churches found throughout New Orleans. Shown here are examples from Sacred Heart, St. Rita, and St. Augustine.

A PELICAN IN HER PIETY
Stallings Hall - Loyola University
6363 St. Charles Avenue - Audubon

This is an interesting variation of the *A Pelican In Her Piety* at Loyola University which includes four baby pelicans in the nest.

SAINT PIO OF PIETRELCINA O.F.M.C.
St. Louis Cemetery #3 - Esplanade Ridge

Padre Pio, Francesco Forgione, was born in 1887. In 1918, Padre Pio (Pius) received the stigmata while kneeling before a crucifix. The stigmata are the five visible wounds suffered by Jesus Christ on the cross, thus making Pio the first stigmatized priest in Church history. The visible wounds stayed with Padre Pio for the rest of his life. In 2002, Padre Pio was canonized by Pope John Paul II, becoming Saint Pio of Pietrelcina. Pio, a member of the Order of Friars Minor Capuchin, died in 1968. The detail on this statue includes the fingerless gloves Pio wore to hide his painful wounds. He is the patron of civil defense volunteers and adolescents.

MARTIN OF CHARITY

Juan Martin de Porres was born of mixed parentage in Peru in 1579. He inherited the dark complexion of his mother resulting in rejection by his Spanish father until he was eight years old. Due to his status as a mulatto, he was not allowed to become a full member of the Dominican Order. Holding the title of lay brother, he was relegated to performing menial tasks around the monastery. Martin spent his time nursing the sick and caring for the poor, while suffering the discrimination and racism thrust upon him by others.

He is often depicted with a broom since he was proud of his labors and believed that all physical work was sacred no matter how menial. In some illustrations, he is accompanied by a dog, a cat, and a mouse all eating from the same bowl as a symbol of interracial harmony.

Martin De Porres died in 1639, and was canonized by Pope John the XXIII in 1962. He is the patron of mixed-race people, the poor, barbers, race relations, and social justice.

"He excused the faults of others. He forgave the bitterest injuries. ... he deserved to be called ... Martin of Charity."
- Pope John the XXIII

SAINT MARTIN DE PORRES O.P.
St. Dominic Catholic Church
775 Harrison Avenue - Lakeview

SAINT MARTIN DE PORRES O.P.
St. Anthony Of Padua Church
4640 Canal Street - Mid-City

DIVINE MATCHMAKER AND HEALER

SAINT RAPHAEL THE ARCHANGEL AND TOBIAS
Our Lady of the Rosary Catholic Church
3368 Esplanade Avenue - Esplanade Ridge

    The Archangel Raphael is depicted here watching over Tobias during a long journey. Raphael's staff appears to be missing from this sculpture. Tobias, travelling with his faithful dog, stopped to rest and wash on the banks of the Tigris River. When a huge fish tried to devour Tobias, Raphael told him to kill it and gave him instructions to create medicine from the entrails. With the medicine, Tobias cured his father's blindness.

*"I am the Angel Raphael,
one of the Seven who stand before the Lord."* - **Tobit 12:15**

SAINT RAPHAEL THE ARCHANGEL AND TOBIAS
The Chapel of St. Michael the Archangel
St. Roch Cemetery #2 - Faubourg St. Roch

Raphael means, *God heals*. He shows compassion to those who are struggling physically or spiritually. St. Raphael is the patron of travelers, physicians, lovers, nurses, shepherds, and those with eye problems.

VIA CRUCIS
STATION XII

Jesus Dies on the Cross

ST. STEPHEN CATHOLIC CHURCH
1025 Napoleon Avenue - Touro

" ... didst Thou hang in agony, and then die for me ..."

THE REDEMPTORISTS

"Copiosa Apud Eum Redemptio"
With Him is Plentiful Redemption

The Congregation of the Most Holy Redeemer is a Catholic missionary congregation founded by St. Alphonsus de' Liguori. Members are known as Redemptorists. The seal consists of a cross resting on three hills. The lance and sponge represent the instruments of The Passion. On either side of the cross are the abbreviated names of Jesus and Mary. Above the cross is the radiant eye of God symbolizing His gracious mercy to humanity. The seal is supported by crossed branches of laurel and palm and surmounted by the Crown of Heavenly Glory. This stained glass transom is from St. Mary's Assumption Church at 919 Josephine Street across from St. Alphonsus.

**THE COAT OF ARMS FOR THE
CONGREGATION OF THE MOST HOLY REDEEMER
St. Alphonsus Catholic Church Narthex
2030 Constance Street - Lower Garden District**

SAINT RITA OF CASCIA
St. Rita of Cascia Catholic Church
2729 Lowerline Street - Marlyville-Fontainebleau

Look closely at this statue of Margherita Lotti and you will see the thorn from Christ's crown that pierced her forehead. This incident of a partial stigmata occurred while Rita was meditating on the crucifix. She was canonized in 1900, and is the patron of impossible causes and wounds.

SAINT ROCH
The Chapel of St. Roch - St. Roch Cemetery #1
The National Shrine of St. Roch
St. Roch at N. Derbigny Street - Faubourg St. Roch

St. Roch is celebrated in New Orleans by way of St. Roch Chapel, St. Roch Cemetery, Faubourg St. Roch, St. Roch Avenue, St. Roch Market, and, of course, St. Roch Tavern.

THE NATIONAL SHRINE OF SAINT ROCH

The Chapel of Saint Roch was erected by a young German priest, Father Peter Leonard Thevis, in response to the intervention of St. Roch during the New Orleans yellow fever epidemic of 1867-68. Thevis is buried in the center aisle near the altar. The cemetery, Campo Santo or *Holy Field*, evolved around the chapel and grew into two sections, including Saint Michael's Chapel and Mausoleum in the rear section.

Saint Roch spent his life attending to the plague-stricken population of Italy. He eventually fell victim to the disease and retreated to the forest to recover in isolation. His likeness is always accompanied by the hunting dog that brought him bread during his illness. His right hand points to the plague sore on his right thigh. St. Roch's iconography also includes scallop shells on his hat and pouch indicating his experiences as a pilgrim. He is the patron of dogs, pilgrims, gravediggers, and victims of epidemics.

THE CHAPEL OF ST. ROCH - ST. ROCH CEMETERY #1
St. Roch at N. Derbigny Street - Faubourg St. Roch

A small room is located just to the right of the altar which has become a shrine containing a remarkable collection of ex-votos including plaster casts of limbs, plaques, and assorted tokens testifying to cures and favors granted by St. Roch.

"Lord, increase my sufferings and with them increase Thy love in my heart." - **Santa Rosa de Lima**

SAINT ROSE OF LIMA T.O.S.D.
St. Rose of Lima Catholic Church - Closed
Bayou Treme Arts and Education Center
2545 Bayou Road - Seventh Ward

Isabel Flores de Olivia was born in Lima, Peru. Her mother witnessed the miracle of a rose blooming on her face as a sleeping child. Isabel took the name of Rosa at her Confirmation. She made her vows and joined the Third Order of St. Dominic. Her self-inflicted suffering included wearing coarse sackcloth studded with nails under her habit. Beneath her veil she wore a spiked crown concealed by beautiful roses. She would often hear a voice cry out to her, *"My cross was yet more painful."* In 1671, she became the first person born in the New World to be canonized by the Catholic Church. Saint Rose is the patron of embroiderers, florists, and gardeners.

VIA CRUCIS
STATION XIII

The Body of Jesus is Taken Down from the Cross

OUR LADY OF PROMPT SUCCOR NATIONAL SHRINE
2635 State Street - Audubon

" ... your suffering and pain are ended ... "

NATIONAL SHRINE OF BLESSED FRANCIS XAVIER SEELOS
"The Cheerful Ascetic"

BLESSED FRANCIS XAVIER SEELOS
St. Mary's Assumption Church
919 Josephine Street - Lower Garden District
Franco Alessandrini - 2001

Knowing it would be his final assignment, Father Francis Xavier Seelos volunteered to serve the people of New Orleans during the yellow fever epidemic of 1867. He was convinced that he would find, "a lasting, resting place at St. Mary's Assumption Church." He diligently served his parish, bringing comfort and solace to the fever-stricken membership as well as to the surrounding neighborhood. Also known as the *Cheerful Ascetic*, this celebrated Redemptorist possessed great mystical gifts due to his intense prayer life. He is credited with many healing miracles during the epidemic as well as intercessions made after his own death from yellow fever in 1867. In 2000, the Catholic Church beatified Father Seelos making him one step away from sainthood. The National Shrine of Blessed Francis Xavier Seelos is located in Saint Mary's Church and contains relics and memorabilia relating to his miraculous life and unselfish death. The shrine remains one of the more popular pilgrimage sites in the world.

"In Cruce Salus" - Salvation From the Cross

URSULINE CONVENT GARDEN
Chartres at Ursulines Street - French Quarter
Franco Alessandrini - 2002

NATIONAL SHRINE OF BLESSED FRANCIS XAVIER SEELOS
919 Josephine Street - Lower Garden District

THE FIRST MARTYR

SAINT STEPHEN
St. Stephen Catholic Church
1025 Napoleon Avenue - Touro

This is one of four stained glass windows featuring events in the life of the first martyr of Christianity. The windows depict his friendship with the poor, his life as the teacher of good news, and Saint Stephen on trial. This fourth window features Stephen's death from stoning while wearing his deacon vestments. St. Stephen is the patron of deacons, masons, altar attendants, and casket makers. He is usually shown carrying three stones, symbols of his martyrdom.

LILY OF THE MOHAWKS

SAINT KATERI TEKAKWITHA
Blessed Francis Xavier Seelos Parish Catholic Church
3053 Dauphine Street - Bywater

Catherine Tekakwitha was an Algonquin-Mohawk virgin and laywoman. She was shunned by her tribe for converting to Catholicism. Tekakwitha was canonized in 2012, and is the patron of Native Americans, ecologists, and the environment.

"If you pray, you will have faith. If you have faith, you will love. If you love, you will serve. If you serve, you will have peace."
- **Mother Teresa**

BLESSED TERESA OF CALCUTTA M.C.
St. Louis Cemetery #3 - Esplanade Ridge

Anjezë Gonxhe Bojaxhiu was born on August 26, 1910, but chose to celebrate her birthday on August 27, the day she was baptized. Mother Teresa founded the Missionaries of Charity which remains active today in 133 countries. She won the Nobel Peace Prize in 1979. Teresa passed away in 1997, and was beatified on October 19, 2003. Bestowed with the title, *Blessed*, she is one step away from canonization.

"Christ has no body but yours, no hands, no feet on earth but yours ..."
- St. Theresa of Ávila

SAINT THERESA OF ÁVILA
St. Theresa of Ávila Catholic Church
1404 Erato Street - Lower Garden District

Teresa Sanchez Cepeda Davila y Ahumada was born in Ávila, Old Castile on March 28, 1515. She is wearing the habit of the Discalced Carmelites, an order of cloistered nuns, which she reformed. A monastery building and chapel of this order is located at 1236 N. Rampart Street in the French Quarter. Theresa is holding a book and a quill. She is celebrated for her contributions to the mystical literature of the Catholic Church.

The modern spelling of her name is *Teresa of Ávila*. She died in 1582, and was canonized in 1622. She is the patron of sick people, lace workers, and members of religious orders.

THE LITTLE FLOWER OF JESUS

SAINT THERESA OF LISIEUX O.C.D.
The Cathedral-Basilica Of St. Louis King Of France
Jackson Square - French Quarter

Theresa loved nature and saw herself as a *small wild flower* in the garden of Jesus, not a beautiful rose or lily. She wrote, " ... *if all flowers wanted to be roses, nature would lose her springtime beauty ... so it is in the world of souls ...* " She saw the roses blooming in the convent garden as she lay dying. She said, *"After my death, I will let fall a shower of roses."* She was canonized in 1925. Pope Pius X called her the greatest saint of modern times. She is the patron of florists, gardeners, and those who lose their parents. The modern spelling of her name is *Therese of Lisieux*.

**ST. THERESA LITTLE FLOWER OF
THE CHILD JESUS CATHOLIC CHURCH
3810 Leonidas Street - Dixon
Entrance Tympanum Detail**

**ST. THERESA
Our Lady Star Of The Sea Catholic Church
1835 St. Roch Avenue - Faubourg St. Roch**

THE HOLY TRINITY

THE OLD TESTAMENT TRINITY
Holy Trinity Greek Orthodox Cathedral
1200 Robert E. Lee Boulevard - Lakeview
Laurence Manos - 1986

This icon of the Old Testament Trinity is referred to as, *The Hospitality of Abraham*. It illustrates the appearance of three angels to Abraham and Sarah at the Oak of Mamre in Genesis 18. They treat the visitors with great reverence by preparing an elaborate meal. When Abraham speaks to them, they respond as one. The center figure represents Christ - *the Word of God*. On the right is the Holy Spirit - *the Breath of God*. They both bow slightly in reverence toward the Father seated at the left of the table.

THE HOLY TRINITY
St. Andrew's Episcopal Church
1031 S. Carrollton Avenue - East Carrollton

There are three ingredients that form the basis of most Creole and Cajun cooking, often referred to as the *holy trinity*. This celebrated New Orleans cooking tradition includes celery, onions, and bell pepper which are usually sautéed together. I thought it appropriate to mention that here.

URSULINES

The Ursuline Nuns from Rouen arrived in New Orleans in 1727, by consent of King Louis XV of France. Fourteen nuns completed the arduous journey to the *mudhole*. Their mission was to establish a hospital and provide educational opportunities for the young women of the colony. The current French Quarter building associated with the Ursulines is a National Historic Landmark and one of the oldest buildings in New Orleans. It was constructed between 1748 and 1752. *"It is the finest surviving example of French Colonial public architecture in the United States,"* according to the National Park Service. It is referred to as the Old Ursuline Convent and later became the Archbishopric, or Archbishop's Palace, when the sisters moved to the Lower Ninth Ward. The entire complex with herb garden, museum, archives, and St. Mary's Church is part of the Catholic Cultural Heritage Center. It is also called the Archbishop Antoine Blanc Memorial Complex. The convent is now located in the Audubon neighborhood of New Orleans along with Ursuline Academy and The National Shrine of Our Lady of Prompt Succor.

THE URSULINE CONVENT
Catholic Cultural Heritage Center - St. Mary's Church
Chartres at Ursulines Street - French Quarter

APOSTLE TO THE FAR EAST

SAINT FRANCIS XAVIER S.J.
Katharine Drexel Preparatory School
Formerly: Xavier University Preparatory School
5116 Magazine Street - West Riverside

Xavier University and Xavier Prep were both named for one of the greatest missionaries since the time of the apostles. This reverent statue of Francisco de Jasso y Azpilicueta rests in a niche above the entrance of St. Katharine Drexel Preparatory School. Saint Xavier and Saint Ignatius of Loyola were co-founders of the Society of Jesus. They were canonized together in 1622. St. Francis Xavier is the patron of foreign missions, missionaries, and navigators.

VIA CRUCIS
STATION XIV

Jesus is Laid in the Tomb

BLESSED FRANCIS XAVIER SEELOS CATHOLIC CHURCH
3053 Dauphine Street - Bywater

" ... I, too, would lie dead; but if I live, let it be for Thee ... "

"OUR LADY OF THE DELUGE"
7000 Bellaire Drive - Lakeview
Facing the 17th Street Canal Floodwall Breach
Photographed: November 2005

BIBLIOGRAPHY

Arthur, Stanley Clisby – Old New Orleans, Harmanson New Orleans, 1936
Castellanos, Henry C. – New Orleans As It Was, 1895
Catholic Cultural Heritage Center, stlouiscathedral dot org
Chase, John – Frenchmen, Desire, Good Children, Pelican Publishing, 2001
Cocke, Edward H. – Monumental New Orleans, Lafayette Publishers, 1969
Comune di Bisaquino – Provincia di Palermo, Sicilia, Italy, palermoweb dot com
Early, Eleanor – New Orleans Holiday, Rinehart & Company, 1947
Ecclesiastical Heraldry, wikipedia dot com
Faith, Hope and Sister Camille Anne, bestofneworleans dot com
Francis Xavier Seelos National Shrine, seelos dot org
Gandolfo, Henri A. – Metairie Cemetery: An Historical Memoir, Stewart Enterprises, 1981
Gill, Donald A. – Stories Behind New Orleans Street Names, Bonus Books Chicago, 1992
Good Friday in New Orleans, nola dot com/religion, 2014
Greater New Orleans Community Data Center, dataresearchcenter dot org
Henriette Delille Prayer Room, stlouiscathedral dot org
Higgins, Earl J. – The Joy of Y'at Catholicism, Pelican Press New Orleans, 2007
History of Our Lady of Guadalupe, judeshrine dot com
How to Recognize the Holy Apostles in Icons:
    A Reader's Guide to Orthodox Icons, iconreader dot wordpress dot com
Huber, Leonard V. – McDowell, Peggy; Christovich, Mary Louise
    New Orleans Architecture: The Cemeteries, Pelican Publishing, 1989
Huber, Leonard V. – Clasped Hands Symbolism in New Orleans Cemeteries,
    The Center for Louisiana Studies, 1982
Il Santuario della Madonna del Balzo, web dot Tiscali dot it/bisaquino
Keister, Douglas – Stories in Stone, Gibbs Smith Publisher, 2004
King, Grace – New Orleans: The Place and the People, Macmillan Company, 1895
Mystical City of God, sacredheart dot com
New Orleans Churches, neworleanschurches dot com
New Orleans Past: WPA In New Orleans, neworleanspast dot com
Nolan, Charles E. – Splendors of Faith, La. State University Press, 2010
Old New Orleans, thepastwhispers dot com
O Regina del Monte Triona, congregazionemadonnadelbalzo dot it
Our Lady of Prompt Succor, ourladyofpromptsuccor dot com
Poor Clare Sisters, poorclare dot org
Robinson, Laura – It's An Old New Orleans Custom, Bonanza Books, 1948
Saint Ann Shrine in New Orleans, louisianafolklife dot org
St. Frances Cabrini Shrine, cabrinihigh dot com
Saint Joseph Altars, catholicreview dot org
Saint Louis King of France, catholic dot org
Saint Roch: Why St. Roch Rolls, myneworleans dot com, 2013
Saint Roch Cemetery, storyvilledistrict dot com/cemeteries
Saints and Spirits, voodoomuseum dot com
Saxon, Lyle; Dreyer, Edward; Tallant, Robert – Gumbo Ya-Ya, Bonanza Books, 1945
Smithsonian Institution Research Information System, siris dot si dot edu
Stall, Gaspar J. "Buddy" – Louisiana COD, Gaspar J. Stall, 2000
Stations of the Cross, catholic dot org
The Papal Visit to New Orleans, September 13, 1987, nytimes dot com
Tomb of the San Bartolomeo Society, ustica dot org/san_bartolomeo
WPA - New Orleans City Guide, Houghton Mifflin, Boston, 1938

ABOUT THE AUTHOR

Kevin J. Bozant was born in the Upper 9th Ward of New Orleans—as luck would have it—just a few blocks from Huerstel's Bar and Little Pete's Seafood Restaurant. He is a local writer, photographer, and graphic designer for his publishing company, Po-Boy Press – New Orleans.

His professional experience includes the local Warner Brothers, CW, and ABC television affiliates. Kevin specialized in color print and electronic graphics for marketing and promotional materials as well as special events coordination. He eventually became senior graphic designer for the news, sports, and weather departments. He provided technical and graphics assistance for Real New Orleans, Crescent City Country, New Orleans After Midnight, Friday Night Football, Saints Sideline, as well as Brandon Tartikoff's popular New Orleans trivia game show, N.O. It Alls. He helped developed and co-produce The Southern Garden for Vitascope Television and created the Crescent City Crier for Gambit Weekly.

Kevin has written a number of guide books exploring and celebrating various aspects of New Orleans history and culture. He also narrates GPS guided walking tours of New Orleans for VoiceMap.

He lives in the Gentilly Terrace and Gardens Neighborhood of New Orleans.

poboypress@yahoo.com

www.amazon.com/author/kevinjbozant

VoiceMap information available at: voicemap.me/authors/kevin-j

Made in the USA
Monee, IL
27 June 2021